The

DUTCH OVEN COOKBOOK

❋

The
DUTCH OVEN
COOKBOOK

Recipes for the Best Pot in Your Kitchen

Sharon Kramis & Julie Kramis Hearne

SASQUATCH BOOKS
SEATTLE

To Marion Cunningham, a great teacher
& good friend.
—S. K. and J. K. H.

Printed in Canada
Published by Sasquatch Books
Distributed by Publishers Group West
15 14 13 12 11 10   9 8 7 6 5

Photography copyright ©2006 by Alex Hayden
Food styling: Christy Nordstrom
Book design: Kate Basart/Union Pageworks

Library of Congress Cataloging-in-Publication Data

Kramis, Sharon.
        The dutch oven cookbook : recipes for the best pot in your kitchen /
        Sharon Kramis & Julie Kramis Hearne.
                p. cm.
        ISBN 1-57061-498-9
        1. Dutch oven cookery. I. Hearne, Julie Kramis. II. Title.

TX840.D88K72 2006
641.5'89--dc22   2006044656

Sasquatch Books
119 South Main Street, Suite 400
Seattle, WA 98104
206/467-4300
www.sasquatchbooks.com / custserv@sasquatchbooks.com

CONTENTS

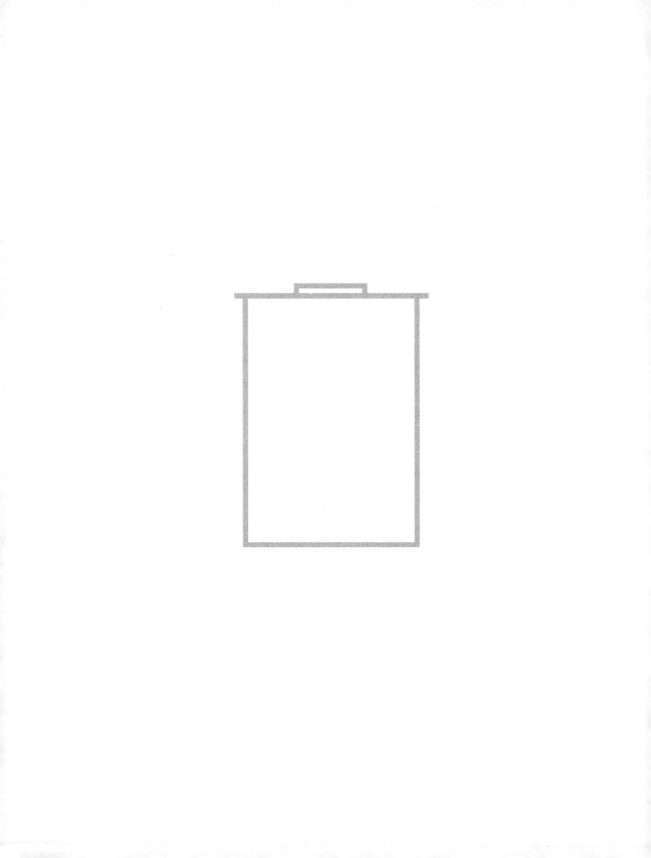

ACKNOWLEDGMENTS

To our family and friends, whom we love to bring together to share good food and good stories. To those who contributed recipes, we are grateful. We want to thank Gary Luke, Chad Haight, and Heidi Schuessler of Sasquatch Books. A special thanks to our very talented photographer, Alex Hayden, and our food stylist, Christy Nordstrom. Also, many thanks to Bob Kellerman and everyone at Lodge Manufacturing in South Pittsburg, Tennessee, for continuing to manufacture (for four generations) cast iron cookware.

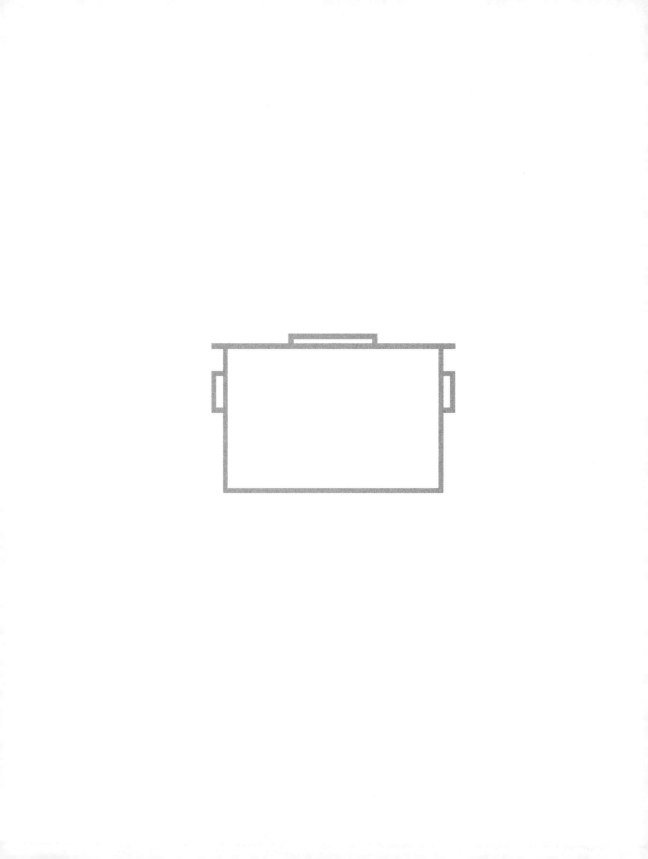

INTRODUCTION

The Dutch oven is our favorite pot. Made of cast iron and often enamel coated, it's the perfect partner to the cast iron skillet—our favorite pan. Dutch ovens have loop handles and flat bottoms, and always come with lids. They are approximately 4 to 5 inches deep and range in capacity from 2 to 13 quarts. The name "Dutch oven" is believed to have originated in the eighteenth century, when the cookware was manufactured in England and brought to the United States by Dutch traders.

Historically, the pot was used primarily outdoors. During the pioneer days in the western United States, for example, Dutch oven cooking was the most important cooking method used. Today, a strong following still cooks with Dutch ovens over a campfire. Throughout the country Dutch Oven Societies sponsor annual outdoor gatherings for recipe sharing and friendly but grueling competitions for a grand prize.

In our cookbook—a collection of our favorite recipes—we are bringing the Dutch oven indoors. Here in the Northwest, after the first rainfall in September, the mushrooms pop up in the forests and the Dutch oven comes out of the cupboard to claim the back burner on the stove, where it remains until mid-April. At least three times a week in our kitchens, something is either stewing, braising, simmering, or roasting in the Dutch oven. A pot of soup on the stove, slowly simmering, was always a welcome-home treat after school.

A heavy pot, the Dutch oven slow-cooks tough meats and melds flavors together to produce melt-in-your-mouth tender bites. Use medium to low heat to attain the best results. We prefer the Dutch oven to Crock-Pot cookery because it slow-cooks without accumulating excess moisture. Some cuts of meat are often overlooked by consumers because of the longer cooking times (2 to 3 hours), even though these cuts can be more flavorful and much less expensive than steaks and chops. Enter the Dutch oven: Slow-cooked recipes simmered on the stovetop or oven-baked in the Dutch oven provide a delicious supper.

Your Dutch Oven

Many people have different ideas of exactly what cooking in a Dutch oven is. For those who cook outdoors with their Dutch oven, there is only one type: the true cast iron pot that does not have an enamel coating and has been in the family forever. Our cookbook, however, is written for indoor cooking in the Dutch oven. For that purpose, there are two basic types of pots: enameled cast iron and nonenameled basic black preseasoned cast iron. We use both types, and each results in slow-cooking and great-tasting food.

Dutch ovens are heavy and they conduct even heat on the sides as well as on the bottom. Stainless-steel pots, Teflon-coated pots, and Crock-Pots don't give you the same delicious results. Those pots tend to accumulate extra moisture. A Dutch oven provides even heat and retains that heat for long periods of time.

Purchasing Dutch Ovens

Our favorite Dutch oven for indoor cooking is an enameled 5- to 6-quart pot. The price range is anywhere from $50 to $250. Today the Lodge Manufacturing Company, a fourth-generation, family-run foundry in South Pittsburg, Tennessee, and the oldest manufacturer in the United States, is producing enamel-coated cast iron. Lodge, Le Creuset, Staub, and Mario Batalli cookware all manufacture quality enamelware that can go from the stovetop directly into the oven. (See Resources, page 141.)

Care and Use of Your Dutch Oven

To ensure a long life for your pot, remember these basic guidelines:

1. Just rinse it out with a little soapy water and a soft sponge. To remove any stuck particles from your Dutch oven, soak the pot in hot soapy water and scrub with a plastic scouring pad. Never use heavy abrasives or metal scouring pads.

2. On the stovetop, cook over low to medium heat. Never use your Dutch oven over high heat for searing, or the enamel will crack and chip.

3. Don't leave an empty pot on a hot burner—the enamel will crack.

4. Please take care not to drop or bang your Dutch oven, as the enamel coating can chip. However, chipping does not make it unsafe to use.

5. Dutch ovens are ovenproof; however, the knobs and handles get hot and stay hot! Be careful! Always use two thick oven mitts when handling your pot.

Cooking with a Dutch Oven

The primary use of the Dutch oven is for slow, even cooking. Its ability to evenly distribute heat on the sides as well as on the bottom makes it the perfect pot for tenderizing and braising tougher cuts of meat. The Dutch oven is easy to clean and compatible with electric, gas, ceramic, and induction ranges. There is something so wonderfully simple and satisfying about meals you cook in one pot. We hope you enjoy these recipes as much as we do!

SOUPS, CHILIES & CHOWDERS

Basic Dutch Oven Bean Soup
Hearty Black Bean Soup
Lentil Sausage Soup
White Bean, Swiss Chard, and Andouille Sausage Soup
Hot and Sour Soup
Lemongrass Chicken Pho
Rotisserie Chicken Noodle Soup
Cock-a-Leekie
Shanghai Dumpling Soup
Late Summer Garden Minestrone
Pasta Fagioli Soup
Ribollita Soup
Provençal Vegetable Soup with Pistou
Tortilla Soup
Roasted Beet Soup
Spring Asparagus Soup with Chives and Crème Fraîche
Wild Mushroom and Barley Soup
Cougar Gold Cheddar Cheese and Potato Soup with Granny Smith Apples
Yukon Gold Potato and Leek Soup
Parsnip, Potato, and Pear Soup
Country French Onion Soup with Golden Gruyère Cheese
Hotel Frontenac Yellow Pea Soup
Kabocha Squash Soup with Toasted Coconut
Seafood Stew in Red Curry Sauce
Simple Curried Lobster Chowder
Chasen's Chili
White Bean and Chicken Chili
TJ's Black Bean and Turkey Chili
Grandpa's French Canadian Chaudiere
Halibut, Corn, and Smoked Salmon Chowder
South Sound Clam Chowder

I

Our motto is "low and slow and let it go." Simmering over low heat in your Dutch oven slowly combines flavors, so it's no surprise that making soup is one of the most common uses for a Dutch oven.

Most soups and chowders share a simple beginning with three basic ingredients—diced carrots, celery, and onions—known as the classic mirepoix. Building on this, add liquid and presoaked dried beans, dried peas, or lentils and, by changing the seasonings, you can enjoy a different soup every day.

We keep chicken broth, dried legumes, and canned tomatoes in our cupboard as well as fresh celery, carrots, and onions in the refrigerator, so that we always have the ingredients for a delicious soup. After the ingredients have been assembled, bring the soup to a boil over medium-high heat. Immediately turn the heat down and simmer for 45 minutes to 1 hour, until all of the ingredients are tender. We recommend simmering with the lid off to prevent excess moisture from dripping back into the soup or chowder, which will change the taste and color.

You'll find a wide variety of soups in this chapter that will fit any occasion. Hearty Black Bean Soup is a warm bowl of comfort, and we love the flavors in the Seafood Stew in Red Curry Sauce. The White Bean, Swiss Chard, and Andouille Sausage Soup is creamy and colorful, while TJ's Black Bean and Turkey Chili will feed a hungry crowd. The Shanghai Dumpling Soup is a good example of how you can use your Dutch oven to create a quick supper, and the Late Summer Garden Minestrone is full of fresh vegetables from the farmers markets. Simmering in your Dutch oven fills your home with savory aromas and stimulates your taste buds for delights to come.

BASIC DUTCH OVEN BEAN SOUP

Black beans, white beans, lentils, and split peas all start with simple beginnings. If the soup gets too thick, just add more broth. We like our bean soups to have a little character, to not be too thick and mushy. The slightly sweet flavor of the carrots and onions combined with the beans and the chicken broth is delicious.

MAKES 6 SERVINGS

2 tablespoons butter (¼ stick) or olive oil

4 medium carrots (about 8 ounces), peeled and diced

1 small yellow onion, peeled and chopped

2 quarts (8 cups) chicken broth

1 cup dried peas or lentils, or presoaked black or white beans

1 small ham hock

⊘ Heat the butter in a 5½-quart Dutch oven over medium heat for 1 minute. Add the carrots and onions and sauté for 5 minutes, stirring several times. Pour in the chicken broth. Add the legumes and the ham hock and cook uncovered for 10 minutes. Turn the heat down to low and simmer partially covered for 45 minutes. Serve with Parmesan Toasts (see recipe on page 116).

Note: The black and white beans need to be presoaked. Pour 2 cups boiling water over 1 cup dried beans and let soak for 1½ hours, then make your soup. The peas and lentils don't need presoaking, but do rinse and sort them—be on the lookout for small pebbles!

HEARTY BLACK BEAN SOUP

This is a great, easy soup recipe. You don't have to soak the beans overnight or for great lengths of time. Rather, bring the beans to a boil for a couple of minutes, then take them off the heat and let them soak for 1½ hours. Sauté the vegetables and assemble the soup. This hearty soup is a wonderful source of protein, and you'll love the oranges in this recipe.

MAKES 8 SERVINGS

11 cups water

2 cups dried black beans

2 cups chicken broth

2 tablespoon olive oil

1 cup chopped yellow onion

3 cloves garlic, peeled and coarsely chopped

1 cup chopped carrots

1 celery stalk, chopped

1½ teaspoons ground coriander

1½ teaspoons ground cumin

¼ teaspoon dried red pepper flakes

1 cinnamon stick

1 bay leaf

2 oranges, peeled and sectioned (cut away the white pith)

½ cup orange juice

1 tablespoon cider vinegar

¼ teaspoon pepper

2 teaspoons lemon juice

Kosher salt to taste

Sour cream, for garnish

⊘ Bring 8 cups of the water and the beans to a boil in a 5½-quart Dutch oven. Boil for 2 minutes then, keeping the lid on, turn off the heat and let sit for 1½ to 2 hours or until the beans are soft. Drain the beans and put them back in the Dutch oven. Bring the remaining 3 cups water and the chicken broth to a boil, each in their own small pot. Add the boiling water and the broth to the beans in the Dutch oven. Bring the beans to a boil over medium-high heat and then simmer, uncovered.

⊘ Meanwhile, heat the olive oil in a sauté pan over medium heat. Cook the onions and the garlic over medium-low heat for 5 minutes. Add the carrots and sauté for 3 minutes. Add the celery, coriander, and cumin and sauté for 3 minutes more.

⊘ Add the vegetable mixture to the Dutch oven and simmer uncovered for 10 minutes. Add the red pepper flakes, cinnamon stick, bay leaf, oranges, orange juice, and pepper and cook for 10 minutes over medium-low heat. Add the lemon juice and season with the kosher salt.

⊘ Serve in bowls and top with sour cream.

Note: If you want to thicken the soup, purée a few cups with a blender. You may also use a hand-held emulsifier: hold it down in the soup and purée to your desired consistency. Do not lift the emulsifier out of the broth while it is running or you can burn yourself with hot soup. Add more liquid if the soup is too thick.

LENTIL SAUSAGE SOUP

There's nothing better than lentil soup, crusty French bread, and sparkling dry cider. Eastern Washington is the country's largest lentil-growing region. Lentils don't need to be presoaked; just simmer with the rest of the ingredients in your Dutch oven. The lentils are a great source of protein, and the carrots add color and texture.

MAKES 8 SERVINGS

I cup dried lentils

2 quarts (8 cups) chicken broth

I cup chopped yellow onion

I clove garlic, peeled and chopped

I bay leaf

I½ cups peeled and chopped carrots

I cup finely chopped celery

8 ounces smoked sausage (about 2 to 3 pieces), halved lengthwise then cut crosswise into ½-inch slices

Salt and pepper to taste

Tabasco garlic pepper sauce (optional, see note)

⌀ Put the lentils, chicken broth, onion, garlic, bay leaf, carrots, and celery in a 5½-quart Dutch oven. Simmer over low heat, uncovered, for 45 minutes. Add the sausage and cook for 10 minutes longer.

⌀ Season with salt and pepper. Serve with crusty French bread and a crisp green salad. Add a dash of Tabasco garlic pepper sauce to taste.

Note: For a vegetarian version of this soup, substitute vegetable broth for the chicken broth and eliminate the sausage. You can find wonderful flavored Tabasco sauces at your local grocery store.

WHITE BEAN, SWISS CHARD, AND ANDOUILLE SAUSAGE SOUP

This is a quick and hearty soup to fix for lunch. The spicy sausage adds the necessary kick. You can also use a less spicy precooked sausage, such as farmer's sausage.

MAKES 6 SERVINGS

2 tablespoons butter

1 cup peeled and diced carrots

1 cup chopped yellow onion

2 cups peeled and diced Yukon Gold potatoes

6 cups chicken broth

Two 14.5-ounce cans cannellini beans, drained

8 ounces precooked andouille sausage (about 2 pieces), halved lengthwise then cut crosswise into ½-inch slices

2 cups Swiss chard, washed and cut into ½-inch strips

Salt and pepper to taste

⊘ Over medium-low heat melt the butter in a 5½-quart Dutch oven. Add the carrots, onions, and potatoes. Sauté briefly. Add the chicken broth and turn the heat down to low. Simmer for 30 minutes, until the carrots and potatoes are soft. Add the cannellini beans and cook for 5 minutes. Add the sausage slices and the Swiss chard. Simmer briefly.

⊘ Serve in shallow soup bowls. Season with salt and pepper.

HOT AND SOUR SOUP

This is a wonderful recipe. A traditional Chinese soup, it has the perfect balance of hot and sour. When someone you know is feeling under the weather, make them this soup. The "hot" comes from sesame and chile oils, which you can adjust to your liking.

MAKES 4 SERVINGS

4 cups chicken broth

½ cup chopped pork

¼ cup chopped bamboo shoots

½ cup fresh shiitake mushrooms, cut into ¼-inch-thick slices

1 cup firm tofu (½ cube), cut into ¼-inch-thick slices

2 tablespoons soy sauce

½ teaspoon white pepper

3 tablespoons rice wine vinegar

1 egg, beaten

2 tablespoons cornstarch, dissolved in 3 tablespoons water

Chopped green onion, for garnish

Toasted sesame oil, for serving (optional)

Chile oil, for serving (optional)

⟢ In a 5½-quart Dutch oven add the chicken broth, pork, bamboo shoots, and mushrooms and bring to a boil over medium-high heat. Cook uncovered for 3 minutes, then add the tofu and cook for 1 more minute. Add the soy sauce, white pepper, rice wine vinegar, and egg and stir. Thicken the soup with the cornstarch and water.

⟢ Serve in soup bowls and sprinkle with the green onion, and offer the sesame oil and chile oil on the side.

LEMONGRASS CHICKEN PHO

We have many pho restaurants in the Northwest. Steaming hot bowls of this delicious Vietnamese soup are the perfect thing for a rainy day. Make a batch at home to enjoy with your family. Serve with the fresh condiments as well as chile-garlic sauce and hoisin sauce to stir into the soup. We like Mae Ploy fish sauce the best.

MAKES 6 TO 8 SERVINGS

8 ounces dried rice noodles

1 stalk lemongrass

3 quarts (12 cups) chicken broth

Four to six ¼-inch slices of peeled fresh ginger

1 medium sweet onion, cut into quarters and thin slices

2 teaspoons sugar

¼ cup Mae Ploy fish sauce (see Resources, page 141)

2 chicken breasts (skinless and boneless), cut into ½-inch by 2-inch strips

Garnishes

½ cup chopped green onion

1 pound fresh bean sprouts

1 bunch fresh Thai basil, chopped

1 lime, cut into wedges

1 jalapeño, stemmed, seeded, and cut into thin slices

Peanuts, coarsely chopped

Chile-garlic sauce

Hoisin sauce

⟃ Soak the noodles in a large bowl of warm water for 30 minutes. Drain in a colander over the sink. Trim the bottom of the lemongrass stalk (approximately ¼ inch) and discard; remove the outer husk and cut the light green interior into ¼-inch slices.

⟃ In a large Dutch oven simmer the chicken broth, lemongrass, ginger, onion, sugar, and fish sauce for 15 minutes. Add the chicken strips and presoaked rice noodles and cook uncovered for 10 more minutes.

⟃ Serve in deep soup bowls accompanied by a platter of green onion, bean sprouts, Thai basil, lime wedges, jalapeños, and peanuts. Let everyone flavor their own soup with chile-garlic sauce or hoisin sauce, and add their own garnishes.

ROTISSERIE CHICKEN NOODLE SOUP

Roasted chicken adds so much flavor to this chicken noodle soup. The meat is removed from the chicken first, then you make the broth by simmering the rest of the chicken in a Dutch oven. Served with crusty bread, this is a perfect meal for a chilly evening. We like to add the chicken pieces just before serving to prevent them from overcooking.

MAKES 8 SERVINGS

1 rotisserie chicken, skin removed

2 quarts (8 cups) cold water

1 quart (4 cups) chicken broth

2 tablespoons butter

1 cup chopped yellow onion

2 cups diced celery

2 cups finely chopped carrots

2 ounces uncooked spiral egg noodles

Salt and pepper to taste

¼ teaspoon dried dill, for garnish

↻ Remove the white meat from the chicken and cut into ½-inch strips. Put the chicken pieces in a covered dish and refrigerate. Meanwhile, place the chicken carcass in a 5½-quart Dutch oven. Add the water and chicken broth. Simmer over low heat for 45 minutes, uncovered.

↻ In a medium-sized saucepan melt the butter over medium heat. Add the onion, celery, and carrots. Sauté briefly.

↻ After the broth has simmered in the Dutch oven for 45 minutes, remove the carcass with a slotted spoon. Add the uncooked noodles and the carrot and onion mixture and bring to a boil. Turn down the heat to medium-low and add the chicken strips.

↻ Season to taste with salt and pepper. Sprinkle the dill over the soup and serve immediately.

THE
DUTCH
OVEN
COOKBOOK

COCK-A-LEEKIE

This classic chicken soup is easy to fix using a fully cooked rotisserie chicken and your favorite premade chicken broth. The leeks melt in your mouth and give it a silky texture.

MAKES 6 SERVINGS

I rotisserie chicken

4 tablespoons butter (½ stick)

3 leeks, well cleaned, halved, and cut into ¼-inch crescents (tender white and light green part only)

2 quarts (8 cups) chicken broth

I bay leaf

¾ cup uncooked barley

Salt and pepper to taste

⊘ Remove the skin and bones from the chicken. Cut the meat into thin strips and reserve until ready to add to the soup; you should have about 5 cups of chicken. (Save the chicken legs for lunch the next day.)

⊘ Melt the butter over medium-low heat in a 5½-quart Dutch oven. Add the leeks. Stir and cook for 5 minutes. Add the chicken broth, bay leaf, and barley. Reduce the heat to low and simmer uncovered for 30 minutes. Add the reserved chicken pieces. Cook for 15 minutes longer, or until the barley is soft.

⊘ Season with salt and pepper. Serve in soup bowls with pumpernickel bread and sweet butter.

SHANGHAI DUMPLING SOUP

Our good friends Vera and Joey Ing in Seattle serve this soup often in their home. It is a perfect Dutch oven soup recipe. With store-bought barbecued pork and frozen dumplings, it is easy to prepare and so soothing on a January day in the Northwest.

MAKES 4 SERVINGS

One 16-ounce package frozen pot stickers (dumplings)

8 cups chicken broth

1 small knob fresh ginger, peeled and sliced into 4 pieces

4 ounces sliced barbecued pork

3 cups thinly sliced Napa cabbage

1 cup sliced shitake mushroom caps

1 cup diced carrots

½ cup chopped green onions

¾ cup thinly sliced snow peas

2 tablespoons soy sauce

1 to 2 teaspoons sugar

1 teaspoon toasted sesame oil

⊘ Bring 8 cups water to a boil in a large pot. Cook the frozen dumplings in the boiling water for about 8 minutes. Drain in a colander over the sink.

⊘ Bring the chicken broth with the ginger to a simmer in a 5½-quart Dutch oven over medium heat, and simmer for 5 minutes. Add the barbecued pork, cabbage, sliced mushrooms, and carrots and cook for 5 minutes uncovered. Add the green onions, snow peas, soy sauce, sugar, and sesame oil and cook for 1 minute. Add the dumplings and cook for 2 more minutes. Serve right away in large soup bowls.

LATE SUMMER GARDEN MINESTRONE

Every Labor Day weekend our garden is bursting with fresh vegetables.
It's time to make minestrone with the bounty. If you don't have your own
garden, visit your nearby farmers market. Invite your friends for an
end-of-summer get-together.

MAKES 6 SERVINGS

¼ cup extra-virgin olive oil

4 strips lean bacon, cut into ½-inch pieces

1 cup finely chopped yellow onion

3 cloves garlic, peeled and minced

2 celery stalks, chopped

4 medium carrots, peeled and halved lengthwise, then cut crosswise into ½-inch slices

2 cups finely shredded green cabbage

2 cups green beans, cut into 1½-inch pieces

One 15-ounce can cannellini beans, well drained

One 28-ounce can chopped tomatoes, with juice

6 cups chicken broth

2 teaspoons dried Italian seasoning

Salt and pepper to taste

¼ cup chopped fresh parsley

½ cup fresh basil, torn into small pieces

Freshly grated Parmesan cheese, for garnish

⊘ Pour the olive oil into a 5½-quart Dutch oven. Add the bacon pieces and cook over low heat for 4 minutes. Add the onion and sauté for 4 to 5 minutes. Stir in the garlic, celery, and carrots and cook for 2 to 3 more minutes. Stir in the cabbage, green beans, and cannellini beans. Add the tomatoes and juice, chicken broth, and Italian seasoning. Simmer uncovered over low heat for 25 minutes. Season with salt and pepper. Stir in the parsley and basil.

⊘ Serve in deep soup bowls and sprinkle with Parmesan. Serve with rustic Italian bread.

PASTA FAGIOLI SOUP

This classic Italian soup is a great alternative to minestrone. It is wonderful topped with toasted pine nuts and pesto. You can make homemade pesto (see recipe on page 117) or buy fresh pesto in the specialty food section of most grocery stores. We love the Swiss chard and the two types of beans in this soup.

MAKES 8 SERVINGS

I quart (4 cups) chicken broth

¾ cup uncooked pasta shells

12 to 14 ounces turkey sausage (about 4 sausages)

I cup water

One 14.5-ounce can Muir Glen stewed fire-roasted tomatoes

2 small zucchini, coarsely chopped

I clove garlic, peeled and minced

I tablespoon chopped fresh basil

I teaspoon finely chopped fresh oregano

I cup canned kidney beans, rinsed and drained

½ cup canned cannellini beans, rinsed and drained

2 cups chopped Swiss chard

Freshly grated Parmesan cheese, for garnish

Pesto (see recipe on page 117), for garnish

- Heat the chicken broth in a large Dutch oven over medium-high heat. Bring to a boil, add the pasta shells, and reduce the heat to a simmer. Meanwhile, in a separate skillet, cook the sausages with the water and cover for 2 to 3 minutes. Lift the lid to turn the sausages over, cover again, and cook for 2 to 3 more minutes. Remove the lid and allow the moisture to evaporate.

- Remove the sausages and cool for a few minutes. Cut the sausages into ½-inch pieces and add to the Dutch oven. Add the tomatoes, zucchini, and garlic and bring to a gentle boil. Cover and simmer for 3 minutes; stir in the basil, oregano, and kidney and cannellini beans. Cover and simmer for 3 to 5 minutes. Add the Swiss chard and cook for 5 more minutes. Ladle into soup bowls.

- Top with Parmesan and swirl in a spoonful of pesto. Serve with rustic Italian bread.

**THE
DUTCH
OVEN
COOKBOOK**

RIBOLLITA SOUP

This is a wonderful, hearty soup from the Tuscan region of Italy. Ribollita means "reboiled" and uses day-old bread for thickening the soup. Reboil any leftover soup the next day, adding more chicken broth if it gets too thick. The olive oil is always drizzled over the soup just before serving.

MAKES 6 TO 8 SERVINGS

2 tablespoons extra-virgin olive oil

1 cup diced yellow onion

2 medium carrots, peeled and diced

2 celery stalks, diced

2 cloves garlic, peeled and minced

One 14.5-ounce can diced tomatoes, drained

6 cups chicken broth

¾ cup red wine

Two 14.5-ounce cans cannellini beans, rinsed and drained

Four ½-inch slices of day-old rustic Italian bread, torn into small cubes

1 bunch Swiss chard, ribs removed and coarsely chopped

Salt and pepper to taste

Dash of grated nutmeg

Freshly grated Parmesan cheese, for garnish

Extra-virgin olive oil, for garnish

⊘ Heat the olive oil in a 5½-quart Dutch oven over medium heat. Add the onions and cook until softened, about 5 minutes. Add the carrots, celery, and garlic and cook for another 5 minutes. Add the tomatoes, chicken broth, red wine, and cannellini beans and simmer uncovered for 10 minutes. Stir in the bread cubes. Add the Swiss chard on top, pushing down with a wooden spoon. Cover and bring to a boil. Uncover, stir, turn down the heat, and simmer for 15 minutes.

⊘ Season with salt, pepper, and nutmeg. Serve in large soup bowls sprinkled with Parmesan and drizzled with a little olive oil.

PROVENÇAL VEGETABLE SOUP WITH PISTOU

This traditional French vegetable soup is served in many small restaurants in Provence, and it's a wonderful dish for early summer. Pistou is the French version of pesto. It's made here from scratch, but to simplify this soup you can easily substitute a store-bought ready-made pesto.

MAKES 6 SERVINGS

- 2 quarts (8 cups) chicken broth
- 2 cups peeled and diced Yukon Gold potatoes
- 2 leeks, well cleaned and cut into thin slices (including some tender green parts)
- I cup chopped yellow onion
- 3 medium carrots, peeled and chopped
- 3 Roma tomatoes, chopped
- 8 ounces green beans, cut into I-inch pieces
- I cup chopped zucchini
- ½ cup uncooked vermicelli pasta, broken into I-inch pieces
- Two I4.5-ounce cans cannellini beans, drained and rinsed

Pistou

- 3 cloves garlic, peeled and chopped
- 2 cups coarsely chopped fresh basil leaves
- ½ cup freshly grated Parmesan cheese
- I½ cups olive oil

- In a 5½-quart Dutch oven heat the chicken broth over medium heat. Add all of the vegetables except the green beans and zucchini. Cover and simmer for 30 minutes. Add the green beans, zucchini, and pasta and cook for I5 more minutes. Add the cannellini beans and cook for 5 minutes.

- Meanwhile, make the pistou. In a food processor add the garlic cloves, basil, Parmesan, and olive oil and process until well blended.

- Ladle the hot vegetable soup into heated bowls and drizzle with the pistou.

TORTILLA SOUP

We like to roast a chicken the night before making Tortilla Soup. You can use the chicken bones to make stock, or you can use free-range chicken broth, available at most grocery stores. This is a twist from standard tortilla soup, and we find it a bit heartier and more flavorful.

MAKES 8 SERVINGS

I tablespoon butter

I tablespoon olive oil

I cup chopped onion

3 garlic cloves, minced

6 cups chicken broth

½ teaspoon cumin powder

½ teaspoon pasilla powder or chili powder

¼ teaspoon ground cinnamon

One 16-ounce can black beans, rinsed and drained

4 cups cooked, shredded chicken

I cup chopped, seeded tomatoes

Juice of I lime

Salt and pepper to taste

¼ cup cilantro sprigs, for garnish

¼ cup green onion, finely chopped, for garnish

I ripe avocado, peeled, pitted, and cut into large cubes, for garnish

½ cup cubed goat feta or feta cheese, for garnish

I lime cut into 6 wedges, for garnish

Tortilla Strips (see recipe below), for garnish

⊘ Heat a 5-quart Dutch oven over medium heat. Add butter and olive oil. Add onion and cook for 4 minutes. Add garlic and cook to just release the flavor (about I minute). Add chicken broth, cumin, pasilla or chili powder, and cinnamon. Bring to a boil, and then reduce heat. Simmer for 10 minutes. Add beans and chicken, and cook for another 5 minutes or until chicken is heated through. Add tomatoes and lime juice.

↺ Season with salt and pepper. Ladle into warm bowls. Serve with cilantro, green onion, avocado, feta, lime wedges, and tortilla strips on the side. Let your guests enjoy creating the finishing touches.

Tortilla Strips

    4 tablespoons olive oil

    2 tortillas, cut into 1-inch by 5-inch pieces

↺ Heat oil in a skillet over medium heat, add tortilla strips, and cook for 3 minutes on each side or until golden brown. Remove with a slotted spoon to a paper towel.

ROASTED BEET SOUP

Roasting beets brings out their color and sweetness, and the result is this beautiful rose-colored soup. Serve with rye bread and a simple green salad.

MAKES 6 SERVINGS

3 large red beets, stemmed

1 pound Italian bulk sausage

1½ cups chopped yellow onion

2 cloves garlic, peeled and minced

8 cups chicken or beef broth

2 cups shredded and chopped cabbage

1 cup peeled and shredded carrots

2 tablespoons red wine vinegar

1 teaspoon sugar

2 tablespoons lemon juice

Salt and pepper to taste

½ cup sour cream, for garnish

1 bunch chives, chopped, for garnish

⊘ Preheat the oven to 400° F. Wrap the beets individually in foil, and roast on a baking sheet for 1 hour. Cool. Slip off the outer skin by pulling gently, and finely dice the beets.

⊘ Over medium heat in a 5½-quart Dutch oven lightly brown the sausage. Add the onions and garlic. Cook for 5 minutes. Add the broth, cabbage, and carrots. Simmer uncovered for 30 minutes. Add the red wine vinegar, sugar, and lemon juice. Season with salt and pepper. Serve in warmed soup bowls, topped with sour cream and chopped chives.

Note: Roasting the beets can be done a day ahead of time. Whenever we bake potatoes, we roast beets at the same time and use them in salads or soup over the next day or two. For a vegetarian version of this soup, leave out the sausage and use vegetable broth instead of chicken or beef broth.

SPRING ASPARAGUS SOUP WITH CHIVES AND CRÈME FRAÎCHE

This is a basic puréed, creamy vegetable soup recipe. For variety, try substituting 4 cups of fresh spring peas for the asparagus. A hand-held emulsifier is now a basic tool to have in your kitchen. It makes puréeing vegetable soups so easy!

MAKES 6 SERVINGS

> 4 tablespoons butter (½ stick)
> I cup finely chopped yellow onion
> 2 to 3 medium Yukon Gold potatoes (about I pound), peeled and cut into I-inch chunks
> 6 cups chicken broth
> I½ pounds asparagus, cut into I-inch pieces (discard the tough ends)
> I cup heavy cream or I cup chicken broth
> Salt and white pepper to taste
> I tablespoon chopped chives, for garnish

↺ Melt the butter in a 5½-quart Dutch oven over medium-low heat. Add the onions and cook for several minutes, until they begin to soften. Add the potatoes and broth and simmer uncovered for 20 minutes, until fork-tender. Add the asparagus and the heavy cream and cook for 5 minutes longer. Season with salt and white pepper.

↺ Using an electric hand-held emulsifier, purée the soup until smooth (or purée in batches in the food processor). Serve in warm soup bowls, garnished with chives.

WILD MUSHROOM AND BARLEY SOUP

My good friend and cookbook author Pat Mozersky makes this soup in early October, at the peak of wild mushroom season. The barley thickens the soup and provides a delicious background for the chanterelles. A hearty soup, it is wonderful served with a simple green salad and French bread.

MAKES 6 TO 8 SERVINGS

> 1 ounce dried porcini mushrooms
>
> 3 tablespoons olive oil
>
> 2 cups chopped celery
>
> 1 cup peeled and diced carrots
>
> 8 ounces fresh chanterelle mushrooms, cleaned and coarsely chopped
>
> One 28-ounce can chopped tomatoes
>
> ¾ cup uncooked barley
>
> 8 to 9 cups chicken broth
>
> ¼ teaspoon crushed red pepper flakes
>
> 2 teaspoons celery seed
>
> ¼ cup chopped fresh celery leaves, for garnish
>
> 3 tablespoons chopped fresh dill, for garnish

◌ In a small bowl soak the dried porcini mushrooms in hot water for 20 minutes. Remove with a slotted spoon and drain on paper towels. Save the soaking water. Chop the rehydrated mushrooms and reserve.

◌ In a 5½-quart Dutch oven over medium heat add the olive oil and sauté the celery, carrots, and chanterelle mushrooms for 2 to 3 minutes. Add the tomatoes, reserved soaking water, barley, chicken broth, red pepper flakes, and celery seed. Turn the heat to low and simmer uncovered for 1 hour, stirring occasionally. If the soup becomes too thick, add more broth.

◌ Serve in deep soup bowls, and sprinkle the celery leaves and dill over the top.

COUGAR GOLD CHEDDAR CHEESE AND POTATO SOUP WITH GRANNY SMITH APPLES

This is a Northwest favorite. Cougar Gold cheese is a delicious, medium-sharp cheddar cheese developed and sold in 30-ounce tins by Washington State University in Pullman (see Resources, page 141). You can substitute any medium-sharp white cheddar cheese.

MAKES 6 SERVINGS

4 tablespoons butter (½ stick)

1 cup chopped yellow onion

¼ cup plus 2 tablespoons all-purpose flour

1 teaspoon dry mustard

4 cups chicken broth

1 cup peeled and grated carrot

3 cups chopped red potatoes

2 cups half-and-half

3 cups grated Cougar Gold cheddar cheese

Salt and pepper to taste

1 Granny Smith apple, cored and chopped, for garnish

꩜ Melt the butter in a 5½-quart Dutch oven over medium-low heat. Add the onion and sauté until soft, for a few minutes. Stir in the ¼ cup flour and dry mustard. Whisk in the chicken broth until smooth. Add the carrots and potatoes. Simmer uncovered over low heat for 30 minutes. Pour in the half-and-half and stir.

꩜ Shake the grated cheese with the remaining flour in a Ziploc bag. Slowly add the floured cheese to the soup, stirring continuously. Season with salt and pepper. Sprinkle each serving with chopped apples.

24

YUKON GOLD POTATO AND LEEK SOUP

This creamy potato soup is easy to prepare and delicious for lunch. The buttery Yukon Gold potatoes add flavor and give the soup a smooth texture.

MAKES 6 SERVINGS

 2 tablespoons butter

 1½ cups well-cleaned and diced leeks (white part only)

 3 to 4 medium Yukon Gold potatoes (about 2 pounds), peeled and diced

 3 to 4 thyme sprigs

 6 cups chicken broth

 ½ cup heavy cream

 Salt and freshly ground black pepper to taste

 ¼ cup finely chopped green onion, for garnish

⊘ Melt the butter in a 5½-quart Dutch oven over low heat. Add the leeks and cook for 5 to 10 minutes, stirring several times. Add the potatoes, thyme, and chicken broth. Simmer uncovered over medium-low heat for 25 minutes. Discard the thyme sprigs. Partially mash the potatoes with a potato masher. Stir in the cream.

⊘ Season with salt and pepper. Sprinkle with the green onions and serve right away in warmed soup bowls.

PARSNIP, POTATO, AND PEAR SOUP

This soup has a wonderful, velvety texture. You do not need heavy cream to make this soup creamy; puréeing the vegetables takes care of that. Finish this soup off with a small drizzle of truffle oil—just the elegant touch that it needs.

MAKES 8 SERVINGS

3 tablespoons butter

2 large leeks, well cleaned and finely chopped (white and pale green parts only)

2 to 3 medium parsnips (about 1½ pounds), peeled, cored, and cut into 1-inch cubes

2 to 3 medium Yukon Gold potatoes (about 1 pound), peeled and coarsely chopped

2½ cups water

2 cups low-sodium chicken broth

¼ cup apple juice

1 ripe Anjou or Bartlett pear, peeled, cored, and chopped

½ teaspoon ground coriander

Salt to taste

⅛ teaspoon white pepper

Chopped chives, for garnish (optional)

4 strips cooked bacon, crumbled, for garnish (optional)

Truffle oil, for garnish (optional)

⊙ Melt the butter in a large Dutch oven over medium heat. Add the leeks, parsnips, and potatoes. Cook for 5 minutes, stirring often. Add ½ cup water. Cover and cook for 15 minutes. Add the chicken broth, the remaining 2 cups water, and apple juice; increase the heat to high and bring to a boil. Turn the heat to low and simmer uncovered until the vegetables are tender, for about 20 minutes. Add the pears and coriander and heat for 3 minutes.

◌ In a standing blender or with a hand-held blender purée the soup. If using a standing blender, purée the soup 2 to 3 cups at a time (about half filled each time). If the soup is too hot, let it cool down a bit first. If you have a hand-held blender or emulsifier, it can be submerged right into the pot. Do not lift the emulsifier out of the pot while it's running. Purée until smooth.

◌ Heat the soup, season with salt and white pepper, and serve in bowls with chives and crispy bacon or just a small drizzle of truffle oil.

Note: If the soup becomes too thick, add another ½ cup water and ½ cup chicken broth. If you want the soup to have more chunks of vegetables, purée only half of the soup.

COUNTRY FRENCH ONION SOUP
WITH GOLDEN GRUYÈRE CHEESE

It's easy to make this delicious onion soup. Hot and hearty, it's a perfect fall supper entrée. Kitchen Bouquet adds a rich flavor. The wonderful aroma of sautéed onions fills the kitchen. For this recipe we prefer using yellow onions, not sweet yellow onions, which have too much moisture to give the flavor you want.

MAKES 4 SERVINGS

4 tablespoons butter (½ stick)

3 large yellow onions, peeled, cut into quarters, and thinly sliced

1 teaspoon sugar

¾ cup white wine

2 quarts (8 cups) chicken broth

1 to 2 teaspoons Worcestershire sauce

1 tablespoon Kitchen Bouquet

Salt and pepper to taste

4 slices (½-inch-thick) toasted French bread

1 to 1½ cups grated Gruyère cheese

4 to 6 tablespoons freshly grated Parmesan cheese

⊘ Melt the butter in a 5½-quart Dutch oven over medium-low heat. Add the onions and cook slowly uncovered for 30 minutes, stirring occasionally. (They will begin to turn a light golden brown.) Add the sugar and wine and simmer for 5 minutes. Add the chicken broth, Worcestershire sauce, and Kitchen Bouquet and cook for 5 minutes more. Season with salt and pepper.

⊘ Preheat the broiler. Ladle the soup into oven-proof serving bowls. Place the soup bowls on a baking sheet. Top each bowl of soup with a piece of toast. Sprinkle the Gruyère and the Parmesan evenly over each slice. Place the soup bowls under the broiler for several minutes, until the cheese starts to bubble and lightly brown. Serve right away!

HOTEL FRONTENAC YELLOW PEA SOUP

Our family roots reach back to Quebec, where cold winters inspired this soup. The ingredients are usually on hand in the cupboard. You can use either dried yellow peas or dried green peas. Serve with crunchy croutons dropped in the soup just before serving.

MAKES 6 SERVINGS

> 2 cups dried yellow or green peas
>
> 2 quarts (8 cups) chicken broth
>
> 2 cups peeled and diced carrot
>
> 1 cup diced yellow onion
>
> 1 cup (about 4 ounces) diced smoked ham
>
> ½ teaspoon ground allspice
>
> Pinch of cloves
>
> Salt and pepper to taste
>
> Croutons, for garnish

⊘ Put the peas in a colander and rinse under running water. Transfer to a 5½-quart Dutch oven. Add the chicken broth, carrots, onions, ham, allspice, and cloves. Simmer uncovered over low heat for 1 hour. Season with salt and pepper. Ladle into warmed soup bowls and top with croutons.

KABOCHA SQUASH SOUP WITH TOASTED COCONUT

Kabocha squash is a dark green turban-shaped squash with bright orange flesh. You can substitute butternut squash, but we love the flavor of Kabocha.

MAKES 6 TO 8 SERVINGS

1 Kabocha squash (about 2½ pounds), halved lengthwise and seeded

4 tablespoons butter (½ stick)

2 leeks, well cleaned and cut into ¼-inch slices

¾ cup chopped yellow onion

6 cups chicken broth

1 teaspoon orange zest

1 teaspoon garam masala (see Resources, page 141)

½ cup coconut milk

1 cup toasted flaked coconut, for garnish (optional)

☉ Preheat the oven to 350° F. Place the squash, cut side down, on a lightly oiled baking sheet and bake for 50 minutes. Cool, then scoop out the squash meat and save.

☉ In a large Dutch oven over medium heat melt the butter. Stir in the leeks and onions. Cook uncovered for 5 minutes, until the leeks soften. Add the squash meat, chicken broth, orange zest, and garam masala. Simmer uncovered over low heat for 30 minutes.

☉ Remove 4 cups of the soup and cool slightly. Purée in a food processor until smooth. Return to the pot. Stir in the coconut milk, heat for 5 minutes, and serve garnished with the toasted coconut flakes.

Note: For a vegetarian version of this soup, substitute vegetable broth for the chicken broth.

SEAFOOD STEW IN RED CURRY SAUCE

This soup, also known as Tom Kai Talay, offers a wonderful balance of heat from the curry and sweetness from the coconut milk. See Resources (page 141) for information on how to order curries and fish sauce if you do not have an Asian or specialty food store in your area.

MAKES 4 SERVINGS

I cup chicken stock

I cup coconut milk with cream on top (the Chaokoh brand is a nice choice)

I tablespoon red curry paste

2 teaspoons brown sugar

3 slices galangal or peeled ginger root (¼ inch by 1 inch)

I fresh lemongrass stalk, outside hull removed, rinsed and cut into ½-inch coins (white part only)

3 dried whole kaffir lime leaves

2 teaspoons fish sauce

8 ounces mussels, well rinsed and debearded just before cooking

8 ounces clams, well rinsed

I pound cod or halibut fillets, cut into 4-inch pieces

I tablespoon lime juice

½ bunch of fresh cilantro sprigs, hand-torn, for garnish

6 to 8 sprigs Thai or locally grown fresh basil, hand-torn, for garnish

I lime, cut into 8 wedges

Diced Thai green chile, for garnish (optional)

❍ Pour the chicken stock into a large Dutch oven. Bring to a boil over medium heat. Add the coconut milk and turn the heat down to medium-low. Whisk in the red curry paste and brown sugar. Add the galangal, lemongrass, and lime leaves and cook uncovered for 5 minutes. Add the fish sauce and stir. Add the mussels, clams, and fish. Be sure to submerge the fish in the broth so it will completely cook and absorb the flavors. Cover and continue to cook for 7 minutes.

❍ Give the pot a brief shake to move the shellfish around. Add the lime juice and serve in shallow bowls with steamed jasmine rice on the side. Accompany with small bowls of cilantro, Thai basil, and lime wedges—and diced Thai green chile if your guests can handle the heat!

SIMPLE CURRIED LOBSTER CHOWDER

This great recipe is an easy substitution for lobster bisque. You do not need to cook down the lobster shells, so it is much less labor intensive. Plus, the curry and turmeric give this chowder nice flavor without taking away from the flavor of the lobster.

MAKES 6 SERVINGS

2 tablespoons butter

1 cup diced yellow onion

1 large carrot, peeled and finely chopped

1 cup finely chopped celery

1 cup white wine

2 cups chicken broth

2 cups clam broth

2 live lobsters (about 1½ pounds each)

1 medium russet potato, peeled and diced

½ teaspoon curry powder

¼ teaspoon ground turmeric

½ cup heavy cream

¼ cup sherry

Salt and pepper to taste

1 tablespoon chopped chives, for garnish

⊙ Melt the butter in a 5½-quart Dutch oven over medium-low heat. Add the onions, carrots, and celery and sauté until the onions become translucent, for about 5 minutes. Add the white wine, chicken broth, and clam broth and bring to a boil.

- Add the lobsters one at a time: put the first lobster in the pot, cover, and cook for 1 minute; then add the second lobster and replace the lid. Cook for 10 minutes. Remove the lobsters to a plate and let cool.

- Add the potato, curry powder, turmeric, cream, and sherry to the Dutch oven and cook uncovered for 10 minutes. Meanwhile, using a rolling pin without handles (French) or a mallet, smack the lobster tails and claws and remove the meat. Coarsely chop, and return the meat to the pot.

- Season with salt and pepper. Sprinkle with chives.

CHASEN'S CHILI

This is the famous chili that Elizabeth Taylor requested when she was on the set of Cleopatra. *We like the chunkiness of the meats and the texture of the beans. It takes longer to cook this than other chili recipes, but it's worth the extra time. Serve with buttered corn bread, hearts of romaine leaves, and sliced apples with blue cheese dressing for dipping.*

MAKES 8 SERVINGS

8 ounces dried pinto beans, rinsed and sorted

2 tablespoons vegetable oil

3 cups chopped yellow onion

4 cloves garlic, peeled and chopped

1 green bell pepper, stemmed, seeded, and chopped

⅓ cup chopped fresh Italian parsley

4 tablespoons butter (½ stick), softened

2 pounds beef chuck roast, trimmed and coarsely chopped into ⅜-inch pieces

1 pound pork shoulder, trimmed and coarsely chopped into ⅜-inch pieces

⅓ cup Gebhardt's chili powder (or your favorite brand)

1 teaspoon ground cumin

One 28-ounce can diced tomatoes, with juice

Sour cream, for garnish

1 cup grated medium-sharp cheddar cheese, for garnish

¼ cup chopped green onions, for garnish

⊘ Put the pinto beans in a medium-sized pan and cover completely with water. Bring to a boil and cook uncovered for 2 minutes. Turn off the heat, cover, and let stand for 1 hour. Drain the beans and rinse in a colander. Add water to cover the beans and simmer over low heat for 1 hour, until they are nice and soft.

❧ While the beans are cooking, prepare the rest of the chili. In a 5½-quart Dutch oven, over medium heat, add the vegetable oil, onions, garlic, green peppers, and parsley. Sauté for 5 minutes, stirring often. Add the butter, let it melt, then add the beef and the pork, a handful at a time, stirring continuously for 5 minutes. Add the chili powder and cumin. Mix well. Add the tomatoes with juice. Cover and simmer over low heat for 1 to 1½ hours, or until the meat is tender. Wrap the lid with a kitchen towel to prevent excess liquid from dripping back into the pot and toughening the meat.

❧ When the beans are fully cooked, drain well in a colander and add them to the chili mixture. If you add the beans before they are fully cooked, the acidity in the tomatoes will harden them.

❧ Serve topped with sour cream, cheddar cheese, and green onions.

WHITE BEAN AND CHICKEN CHILI

Chilies and chowders are the mainstays of winter Dutch oven cooking. A favorite recipe from the 1980s, this chili is still a must-have for your own collection. Today, it's made even easier when you use a store-bought rotisserie roasted chicken. Serve with warm cornbread and garnish with sour cream, grated Monterey Jack cheese, and salsa.

MAKES 8 SERVINGS

 1 rotisserie chicken
 2 tablespoons extra-virgin olive oil
 2 cups chopped yellow onion
 Three 15-ounce cans cannellini beans, rinsed and drained
 8 cups chicken broth
 One 4-ounce can diced green chiles
 2 cloves garlic, peeled and minced
 2 teaspoons ground cumin
 1½ teaspoons crushed dried oregano
 ¼ teaspoon crushed red pepper flakes
 Salt and pepper to taste
 Sour cream, for garnish
 Grated Monterey Jack, for garnish
 Salsa, for garnish

- Remove the skin and bones from the chicken. Cut the meat into small pieces and reserve until ready to add to the soup.

- Heat the olive oil in a 5½-quart Dutch oven over medium heat. Add the onions and cook for 5 minutes. Add the beans and the chicken broth and cook for 5 minutes. Turn down the heat to low. Add the chicken, green chiles, garlic, cumin, oregano, and red pepper flakes. Simmer uncovered for 20 minutes. Season with salt and pepper.

- Serve warm in deep soup bowls, garnished with sour cream, Monterey Jack cheese, and salsa.

TJ'S BLACK BEAN AND TURKEY CHILI

Our good friend Terry Jarvis and his wife, Cherry, love to cook and entertain friends, and this is one of their favorite recipes. The ground turkey is essentially grease-free and much leaner than ground beef. This thick chili is so good you will want to share the recipe with all of your friends. Serve with warm cornbread.

MAKES 8 SERVINGS

¼ cup olive oil

1 cup peeled and finely diced yellow onion

5 cloves garlic, peeled and minced

1½ pounds ground turkey

1 red bell pepper, stemmed, seeded, and finely chopped

1 cup diced celery

One 12-ounce jar of your favorite salsa

One 28-ounce can plum tomatoes with sauce (break up the tomatoes with your fingers)

Two 14.5-ounce cans black beans, rinsed and drained

One 14.5-ounce can corn, drained

½ teaspoon chili powder

¼ teaspoon ground cumin

Salt and pepper to taste

Grated pepper Jack cheese, for garnish

⊘ Heat the olive oil with the onions and garlic in a 5½-quart Dutch oven over medium heat. Cook for 5 minutes. Add the ground turkey and brown lightly, crumbling with a fork as it cooks. Add the red pepper and celery. Then add the salsa and simmer uncovered for 5 minutes. Add the tomatoes with sauce, black beans, corn, chili powder, and cumin.

⊘ Season with salt and pepper. Serve in warmed soup bowls and sprinkle with the pepper Jack cheese.

GRANDPA'S FRENCH CANADIAN CHAUDIERE

The word "chowder" is derived from the French word "chaudiere" meaning "kettle." It is built in layers, with ingredients added according to the cooking time required. Simmered over low heat, a chowder is a one-pot, one-dish meal.

MAKES 4 SERVINGS

2 strips thick bacon, cut into ½-inch slices

½ yellow onion, peeled and chopped

1 medium russet potato, peeled and cut into 1-inch chunks

1 cup water

1½ cups half-and-half

8 ounces fresh, firm white fish (such as cod or halibut), cut into 2-inch pieces

Salt and pepper to taste

1 tablespoon chopped fresh parsley, for garnish

Several sprigs of finely chopped fresh thyme, or ¼ teaspoon dried thyme, for garnish

⊙ In a 3½-quart Dutch oven sauté the bacon for several minutes over medium heat. Add the onions. Cook uncovered for 5 minutes, stirring occasionally. Add the potato chunks and the water. Cover and simmer over low heat until the potatoes melt, 30 to 40 minutes. Add the half-and-half. When heated, add the fish, cover, and cook for 10 minutes.

⊙ Season with salt and pepper. Serve sprinkled with parsley and thyme.

HALIBUT, CORN, AND SMOKED SALMON CHOWDER

This delicious chowder may be served as an entrée. Enjoy with a basket of hot buttered toast and a crisp apple salad. The smoked salmon adds a nice smoky flavor. Fresh halibut season begins in March and continues into November.

MAKES 4 SERVINGS

3 tablespoons butter

I cup diced yellow onion

I cup finely chopped celery

I fennel bulb, cut into thin strips, white part only (about I cup)

3 tablespoons all-purpose flour

4 cups chicken stock

I bay leaf

1½ pounds small red-skinned potatoes, cut into ¼-inch pieces (about 4 cups)

One 14.5-ounce can corn, drained

I cup heavy cream

4 ounces smoked salmon, crumbled

I pound halibut fillets, cut into 1½-inch pieces

Salt and pepper to taste

2 tablespoons chopped fresh dill, for garnish

⊘ Melt the butter in a 5½-quart Dutch oven over medium heat. Add the onions, celery, and fennel and cook uncovered for 5 minutes. Sprinkle the flour over the vegetables and mix well. Slowly pour in the chicken stock. Cook for 5 minutes, stirring, then turn the heat down to a simmer. Add the bay leaf and the potatoes. Cook over low heat until the potatoes are tender, about 15 minutes. Add the corn. Stir in the heavy cream. Add the smoked salmon and the halibut and gently simmer 8 minutes longer.

⊘ Season with salt and pepper. Serve in warm, shallow soup bowls. Sprinkle the dill over the top.

SOUTH SOUND CLAM CHOWDER

The southern Puget Sound region of the Pacific Northwest is one of the largest shellfish-producing areas in the country. At our family vacation home on Hammersley Inlet, we can dig a bucket of clams in no time and produce this chowder, thickened with crushed soda crackers. If fresh clams aren't available in your area, substitute canned clams and clam juice.

MAKES 6 SERVINGS

2 pounds small Manila clams, well rinsed

1 cup water

1 cup white wine

4 tablespoons butter (½ stick)

1 cup chopped yellow onion

1 cup diced celery

6 cups finely diced red potatoes

1 tablespoon finely chopped fresh thyme leaves

1 quart (4 cups) half-and-half

1 cup crushed soda crackers (crush in a food processor)

1 cup finely diced cooked bacon, for garnish

¼ cup minced parsley, for garnish

Freshly ground black pepper to taste

⟳ Put the clams in a 5½-quart Dutch oven. Pour in the water and wine. Cover. Bring to a boil, turn the heat down to medium, and cook for 5 minutes. Remove the clams with a large strainer. Strain the liquid through a coffee filter and reserve for the chowder. When the clams have cooled enough to handle, remove from the shells and set aside.

⊘ Melt the butter in the Dutch oven over medium-low heat and add the onion, celery, potatoes, and thyme. Sauté over medium heat for 3 minutes. Add the reserved clam juice and the half-and-half. Simmer over low heat until the potatoes are tender. Thicken the broth to the desired consistency by stirring in the crushed soda crackers, a little at a time. Add the clams (no shells).

⊘ Serve right away in warmed soup bowls. Sprinkle each serving with bacon, parsley, and pepper.

**THE
DUTCH
OVEN
COOKBOOK**

SIDES & APPETIZERS

Golden Walla Walla Onion Rings
Fried Five-Spice Baby Back Ribs
Spicy Roasted Clams with Andouille Sausage
Sicilian Antipasto
Navajo Fry Bread
1-2-3 Polenta
Reideralp Swiss Fondue
Spaetzle
Maple-Glazed Roasted Root Vegetables
Roasted Kabocha Squash
Dutch Oven Scrambled Eggs
Farmer's Oven-Baked Potatoes
Risotto
Risi Bisi (Rice and Peas)
Laqua Family Slow-Cooked Beans
Trinity Alps Baked Beans
Bay Braised Artichokes
Tricolor Stuffed Peppers with Sausage
Braised Greens with Smoked Sausage
Sweet and Sour Braised Red Cabbage
Colcannon

The recipes in this chapter call for a variety of Dutch oven sizes: 5½ quarts, 3½ quarts, and 2 quarts. We've found that the dishes turn out best if you use an enameled Dutch oven. Once you start cooking in enameled ironware you will discover why we like it so much. It's the perfect pot for cooking creamy risottos and smooth polenta—no sticking to the bottom of the pot. For example, the Laqua Family Slow-Cooked Beans cook evenly in the 5½-quart pot; the beans get soft and absorb all of the flavors.

The brightly colored enameled Dutch ovens make attractive serving dishes, so you can often cook and serve in the same pot. The Dutch oven will hold its heat and keep your dishes warm. The Spicy Roasted Clams with Andouille Sausage can come right to the table. Be sure to always set your Dutch oven on a trivet or a heavy pot holder to prevent a burn mark on your table.

When you are frying in the Dutch oven, remember that it holds heat well, so when you reach the frying temperature that the recipe calls for, turn the heat down to medium-low to keep the oil from getting too hot.

GOLDEN WALLA WALLA ONION RINGS

A platter of onion rings is meant to be shared. As a favorite fried indulgence, they are hard to resist. Your guests will enjoy the opportunity to eat just one or two of these delicious, salty rings.

MAKES 4 TO 6 SERVINGS

3 large Walla Walla (or Vidalia) sweet onions, peeled and cut into ½-inch-thick slices

1 egg, separated

1 cup milk

1 tablespoon plus 2 quarts (8 cups) vegetable oil for deep-frying

¾ cup plus 2 tablespoons all-purpose flour

2 teaspoons salt

1½ teaspoons baking powder

Sea salt, for sprinkling

⊘ Separate the onions into rings. Cover with cold water for 30 minutes. Drain well on paper towels. In a large bowl mix together the egg yolk, milk, and 1 tablespoon vegetable oil. In a medium-sized bowl mix together the flour, salt, and baking powder and add to the liquid mixture, blending into a smooth batter.

⊘ Heat the remaining vegetable oil in a 5½-quart Dutch oven over medium heat to 360° F. Meanwhile, beat the egg white until stiff and fold into the batter. Dip the onion rings into the batter and fry in the hot oil until golden, turning once. Drain on paper towels and sprinkle with sea salt. Serve right away!

FRIED FIVE-SPICE BABY BACK RIBS

You can bake the ribs ahead of time and fry just before serving. After frying, these ribs get golden brown and crispy on the outside but are melt-in-your-mouth tender on the inside. The five-spice powder and salt add just the right flavor. Watch how quickly they disappear!

MAKES 6 SERVINGS

> 2 racks baby back ribs (about 3½ pounds), rinsed and patted dry, with sinew removed
>
> Salt and pepper for seasoning
>
> 1 cup water
>
> 2 cups peanut or vegetable oil, for deep-frying
>
> 2 tablespoons Chinese five-spice powder
>
> 1 teaspoon salt

- Preheat the oven to 375° F.

- Season the ribs lightly with salt and pepper. Place each rack on a piece of heavy-duty foil larger than the ribs, then place the ribs side by side on a baking sheet and crimp the foil tightly around the ribs, leaving the top open slightly. Pour in the water and place in the oven. Bake for 1 hour. Remove from the oven and open the crimped foil to cool enough to cut the racks into individual ribs.

- Heat the oil in a large Dutch oven to 360° F (until a small sprinkle of flour instantly bubbles). Deep-fry 4 to 5 ribs at a time, about 3 minutes on each side or until they are browned. Remove with long tongs to a platter lined with paper towels.

- In a small bowl, mix together the Chinese five-spice powder and salt. Put the spare ribs in a large paper bag, sprinkle the five-spice mixture over the ribs, and shake the bag 5 times or until the ribs are coated with the spices. Remove the ribs from the bag and serve on a large platter.

Note: Don't discard the oil until it has cooled.

SPICY ROASTED CLAMS WITH ANDOUILLE SAUSAGE

Clams and sausage are a combination often used in Spanish and Portuguese cooking, and this dish makes a hearty meal. Fresh clams are best in this recipe. Dig your own or buy them from your favorite seafood store. The rest of the ingredients are easy to keep on hand.

MAKES 6 SERVINGS

4 tablespoons butter (½ stick)

½ cup diced yellow onion

3 cloves garlic, peeled and minced

8 ounces andouille sausage (about 2 pieces), cut into ¼-inch slices

2 pounds fresh Manila clams, well rinsed

½ cup white wine

One 14.5-ounce can Muir Glen diced fire-roasted tomatoes, drained

1 cup chicken broth

Tabasco sauce to taste

Chopped fresh parsley, for garnish

☺ Melt the butter in a 5½-quart Dutch oven over medium heat. Add the onions and garlic. Stir and sauté for several minutes. Add the sausage slices and cook for 2 minutes, then add the clams and the wine. Cover and cook for 3 to 4 minutes, until the clams have opened. Add the tomatoes and chicken broth. Simmer uncovered for 5 minutes.

☺ Season to taste with Tabasco sauce. Serve in warmed soup bowls and sprinkle with parsley.

Note: If you substitute chorizo, cooked and drained, for the andouille sausage and fresh cilantro for the parsley, you will have a completely new and different, flavorful bowl of clams.

THE
DUTCH
OVEN
COOKBOOK

SICILIAN ANTIPASTO

This is a recipe from Loni Kuhn, a wonderful San Francisco cooking teacher. Her recipes are always favorites whenever they are served. Serve as an accompaniment to a platter of sliced cold roast pork or roast chicken. Pack in your picnic basket with sliced meats, cheese, and a baguette. It keeps well refrigerated.

MAKES 8 TO 12 SERVINGS

¼ cup olive oil

I cup diced celery

1½ cups peeled and diced carrots

2½ cups diced yellow onion

6 cloves garlic, peeled and minced

4 cups sliced cauliflower florets

2 cups diced firm zucchini (the smaller the better)

Two 6-ounce cans tomato sauce

¼ cup tomato paste

¼ cup small capers

Two 8-ounce jars pearl onions, drained

½ cup chopped sweet pickle

½ cup chopped kalamata olives

I cup sliced pimento-stuffed green olives

Two 2-ounce jars quartered olive oil marinated artichoke hearts, undrained

½ cup red wine vinegar

¼ cup sugar

I small tin anchovy fillets, drained and chopped

I cup chopped fresh basil

½ cup chopped fresh parsley

⊘ Pour the olive oil into an enameled 5½-quart Dutch oven over medium heat. Add the celery, carrots, onion, garlic, and cauliflower, cover, and braise in the oil for 5 minutes. Add the zucchini, cover, and steam for 3 minutes more. Mix in the tomato sauce, tomato paste, capers, pearl onions, sweet pickle, kalamata and green olives, artichoke hearts, red wine vinegar, sugar, and anchovy fillets. Cook uncovered for 5 minutes.

⊘ Refrigerate for several days before serving to let the flavors mingle together. Add the basil and parsley just before serving.

NAVAJO FRY BREAD

You can do many different things with fry bread. We like it savory (topped with ground beef, cheese, tomatoes, lettuce, and sour cream) or made sweet (sprinkled with cinnamon and sugar or powdered sugar, or drizzled with honey). You can also make this recipe as an appetizer by forming the bread into small rounds, frying it, and topping it with crème fraîche, smoked salmon, and chopped chives.

MAKES 6 SERVINGS

2 cups all-purpose flour

½ cup instant nonfat dry milk

I tablespoon baking powder

½ teaspoon salt

2 tablespoons shortening

¾ cup water

6 cups vegetable oil, for deep-frying

⌁ Preheat the oven to 200° F.

⌁ In a medium bowl mix together the flour, instant nonfat dry milk, baking powder, and salt. Add the shortening. Rub the mixture with your fingers until coarse crumbs form. Add the water and stir with a fork until the dough comes together. Put the dough on a lightly floured board. Knead until smooth, for about 2 to 3 minutes. Divide the dough into 6 equal portions. Keep it covered in plastic wrap. Shape a portion of dough into a ball, then pat it out on the floured board to make a 6- to 7-inch round. Cover with plastic wrap and repeat to shape the remaining portions. You can stack the rounds of dough with plastic wrap or parchment paper in between them.

⊘ In a 5½-quart Dutch oven heat 2 inches of vegetable oil to 375° F. Turning once, cook each round of dough in the oil until it is puffy and golden brown (about 2 minutes). Line two baking sheets with several layers of paper towels, put the bread in a single layer on paper towels, and keep warm in the oven until all the dough balls are cooked.

⊘ If you make this fry bread ahead of time, let it cool as fried, then package it in an airtight container. Rewarm in a 375° F oven until hot, about 5 minutes.

Lemongrass Chicken Pho,
pages 10–11

Tortilla Soup, *pages 19–20*

Roasted Beet Soup,
page 21

Country French Onion Soup with
Golden Gruyère Cheese, *page 28*

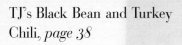

TJ's Black Bean and Turkey
Chili, *page 38*

Halibut, Corn, and Smoked
Salmon Chowder, *page 40*

Navajo Fry Bread,
pages 51–52

Roasted Kabocha Squash,
page 57

Risotto, *page 60*

Tricolor Stuffed Peppers with
Sausage, *page 65*

Smoked Sausage, Chicken, and Shrimp Gumbo, *pages 82–83*

Calcutta Chicken Curry, *pages 84–85*

Baked Short Ribs with Pasilla Pepper Sauce, *pages 96–97*

Bonnie's Fish Stew,
page 110

Roasted Red Pears,
page 129

Beignets, *page 140*

1-2-3 POLENTA

The Dutch oven makes perfect polenta and it's so easy—no spattering, no sticking, so creamy and smooth. We like to use water, a little salt, and Bob's Red Mill coarse grind cornmeal (see Resources, page 141) for its texture. This is the perfect accompaniment to a ragù sauce, such as Ginny Grossi's Ragù Sauce.

MAKES 6 TO 8 SERVINGS

6 cups cold water

1½ teaspoons salt

1½ cups coarse grind cornmeal

4 cups Ginny Grossi's Ragù Sauce (page 114), or 1 jar of your favorite brand

Freshly grated Parmesan cheese, for serving

In a 5½-quart Dutch oven heat the water over high heat. Add the salt and sprinkle the cornmeal into the boiling water, whisking as you pour. Stir and cook for 5 minutes. Turn the heat down to medium and cook for 10 minutes, stirring frequently. Turn the heat down to low and simmer for 15 minutes longer. The polenta will go *plop, plop, plop,* and small volcanoes of steam will begin to appear. Remove from the heat and cover to keep warm.

Serve in warm, shallow bowls, topped with the sauce and sprinkled with Parmesan.

Note: If you don't plan to serve the polenta right away, you can make it and, while it is still hot, spoon the polenta into 12 individual muffin cups. Cover them with plastic wrap and refrigerate. Microwave to reheat, and serve with your favorite tomato, meat, or vegetable sauce.

For an easy baked polenta option: Stir 2 cups cornmeal into 8 cups cold water. Pour into a buttered 9- by 13-inch glass baking dish and bake for 30 minutes at 350° F. Stir in 2 tablespoons butter and bake for another 25 minutes.

REIDERALP SWISS FONDUE

Our Swiss cousins serve this at their chalet in the Alps. The 2-quart Dutch oven makes a great fondue pot. Set on a low-heat warmer and serve with sliced apples and chunks of French bread cut into 1-inch cubes. Offer chilled white wine and apple cider with your fondue.

MAKES 6 TO 8 SERVINGS

8 ounces Emmenthaler cheese, grated (about 2 cups)

8 ounces Gruyère cheese, grated (about 2 cups)

2 tablespoons cornstarch

1 cup dry white wine

1 tablespoon kirschwasser (available at most liquor stores)

Sliced apples and cubed bread, for serving

- In a large bowl, mix the two cheeses and the cornstarch with a wooden spoon. Pour the wine and kirschwasser into a 2-quart Dutch oven and bring to a gentle simmer over medium-low heat. Add the cheese mixture to the wine, a handful at a time, and stir until all the cheese is melted.

- On your dining room table, place the Dutch oven on a small warmer over low heat. With a fondue fork, stab a cube of bread or slice of apple and dip into the melted cheese. If you lose the bread in the fondue pot, you have to kiss the person next to you.

SPAETZLE

You need to have a special piece of equipment to make your own spaetzle, but it's worth the investment. You can make these squiggly noodles quickly, and they can be made ahead of time. You can find a spaetzle maker at cookware shops for $20 to $30. If you have a nice pot roast slow-cooking in your Dutch oven, this is the perfect accompaniment. The spaetzle will soak up the flavorful juices.

MAKES 4 SERVINGS

> 2 cups all-purpose flour
>
> 3 large eggs
>
> ½ cup whole milk
>
> I teaspoon kosher salt
>
> 4 tablespoons butter (½ stick), melted
>
> Salt and freshly cracked pepper to taste

◌ Fill a 5½-quart Dutch oven with water and bring it to a boil over medium-high heat. In a medium-sized bowl mix together with a fork the flour, eggs, milk, and salt. Put ½ cup of the noodle dough into the spaetzle maker. Firmly squeeze the squiggly noodles into the boiling water. Use a knife to cut away any remaining noodles. Cook for 2 minutes. Remove the noodles from the water with a large slotted spoon and put them in a colander to drain. Continue this process until all of the dough is gone.

◌ Transfer the spaetzle to a medium-sized glass baking dish and mix with the butter. Season with salt and pepper. When ready to serve, reheat in the microwave or in a 10- or 12-inch skillet over low heat.

MAPLE-GLAZED ROASTED ROOT VEGETABLES

These vegetables are wonderful roasted together. Each has its own characteristic taste and texture. The spiciness with the sweetness keeps you coming back for more. Even the kids will want seconds! Serve with roast chicken or grilled fish.

MAKES 6 TO 8 SERVINGS

I medium sweet potato, peeled and cubed

2 medium parsnips, peeled, halved, and cut at an angle in I-inch slices

2 medium turnips, peeled and stemmed

2 large carrots, peeled, stemmed, and cubed

4 large shallots, peeled, stemmed, and halved

3 tablespoons olive oil

3 tablespoons maple syrup

3 tablespoons brown sugar

½ teaspoon grated nutmeg

I teaspoon garam masala (see Resources, page I4I)

Salt and pepper to taste

- Preheat the oven to 400° F.

- In a large bowl toss the sweet potato, parsnips, turnips, carrots, and shallots with the olive oil, maple syrup, brown sugar, nutmeg, garam masala, salt, and pepper. Pour the vegetable mixture into a 5½-quart Dutch oven. Place the pot in the oven and roast uncovered for 30 minutes, or until fork-tender. Serve right away.

ROASTED KABOCHA SQUASH

This recipe came together in December, at the end of our farmers market season (it opens again in mid-April). We wanted to see what was available this time of year, and they had Kabocha squash, jumbo fresh-picked Bosc pears, and jumbo walnuts. We couldn't resist the idea of serving this with a roast chicken. The Dutch oven acts like an oven within an oven. It roasts and steams the squash, preventing the dish from drying out.

MAKES 8 SERVINGS

- 1 Kabocha squash, stemmed
- 3 Bosc pears, peeled, cored, and coarsely chopped
- ¼ teaspoon grated nutmeg
- 5 tablespoons butter, melted
- ¼ cup brown sugar
- ¼ teaspoon kosher salt
- 1 cup apple juice or cider
- ½ cup cranberry sauce
- 2 ounces walnuts (about ½ cup coarsely chopped)

- Preheat the oven to 375° F.

- To seed the squash, use one hand to hold it steady and the other hand to carefully stick the knife into the center of the squash. Slowly rock or wiggle your knife into the squash on one side, from top to bottom. Turn the squash over and follow the line to the top of the squash, making a complete cut through the squash. Use a fork or dinner knife to pry the squash open. Remove the seeds. Quarter the squash, always putting the flat flesh side down when cutting. Cut each quarter in half crosswise so you have eight crescent-shaped pieces.

- Add the squash to a 5½-quart Dutch oven; add the pears on top of the slices of squash. Sprinkle the nutmeg over the pears, and drizzle with melted butter. Distribute the brown sugar and salt. Pour in the apple juice.

- Cover and bake for 50 minutes. Remove from the oven, add 1 tablespoon of cranberry sauce and chopped walnuts to each piece, and serve.

DUTCH OVEN SCRAMBLED EGGS

Scrambled eggs are one of the simplest things to make and yet one of the hardest to cook right. These scrambled eggs are not made in a frying pan but in a 2-quart Dutch oven—and they turn out creamy and delicious. Have your sausages or bacon already cooked and held in the oven, and then serve with your favorite coffee cake.

MAKES 4 SERVINGS

> 2 tablespoons butter (¼ stick)
> 6 large eggs, well beaten
> 1½ ounces cream cheese, room temperature
> Salt and pepper to taste

☾ Melt the butter in a 2-quart Dutch oven over medium-low heat. Pour in the eggs. With a heatproof spatula, gently stir the eggs, using an up-and-over motion. Be sure to lift the cooked eggs from the bottom of the pot.

☾ When the eggs are halfway cooked, stir in the cream cheese. Continue to cook, lifting the cooked eggs to the top. Remove from the heat just before the eggs are completely cooked (they'll continue to cook for a minute or two off the heat).

☾ Season with salt and pepper and serve right away. (Soak the pan in a bit of soapy water to clean it. Yes, the eggs stick a little, but it's worth it for the creamy texture you'll get!)

Note: The eggs should only cook for 3 to 5 minutes. It's important to continuously stir and lift the eggs the whole time they are cooking. To prevent the eggs from drying out, don't salt them until they are fully cooked.

**THE
DUTCH
OVEN
COOKBOOK**

FARMER'S OVEN-BAKED POTATOES

This is a tasty side dish to accompany roast pork or chicken. Potatoes, bacon, and onions—how can you go wrong?

MAKES 6 SERVINGS

> 6 to 8 medium-large Yukon Gold potatoes (about 2 pounds), peeled and cut into ½-inch-thick slices
>
> 3 tablespoons olive oil
>
> 4 tablespoons butter (½ stick)
>
> 4 ounces smoked bacon, cut into ½-inch-thick strips
>
> 2 large onions, cut into thin slices
>
> Salt and pepper to taste

⊘ Preheat the oven to 375° F.

⊘ Bring plenty of cold salted water to a boil in a large pot. Add the potatoes and boil for 3 minutes. Drain in a colander and let them dry.

⊘ In a 5½-quart Dutch oven, add the potatoes and gently coat with the olive oil. Cover and bake for 30 minutes.

⊘ Meanwhile, heat the butter in a 10- or 12-inch skillet, add the bacon and onions, and cook for about 5 minutes, or until the onions are soft. Add the mixture to the potatoes and gently mix. Season with salt and pepper. Continue baking uncovered for another 30 minutes. Serve while warm.

RISOTTO

You can get creative with this straightforward risotto recipe. About 20 minutes into cooking, you can stir in such raw ingredients as garden peas and asparagus tips. Or oven-roast beets, coarsely chop them, and add them to the risotto at the end. Fresh shellfish and a little pesto swirled into the risotto is also delicious. We sometimes add a squeeze of lemon juice at the end for a little extra flavor. The finished risotto should be creamy and moist.

MAKES 4 SERVINGS

6 tablespoons butter

½ cup finely chopped yellow onion

2 to 2½ cups chicken broth or beef broth

1 cup short-grain rice (such as Italian arborio rice)

⅓ cup dry white wine

½ cup finely grated Parmesan cheese

⊘ Melt 4 tablespoons of the butter in a 3½-quart Dutch oven over medium-low heat. Add the onion and sauté, stirring until soft and golden. In a separate pot bring the broth to a boil, then turn the heat down to low.

⊘ Add the rice to the Dutch oven with the onions, stirring until all of the grains are well coated with butter. Add ½ cup of the hot broth, stir well, and cook over medium-low heat for 3 to 5 minutes. Continue to add the broth to the Dutch oven, ½ cup by ½ cup, letting it cook away after each addition and stirring continuously to prevent the rice from sticking to the pot. (Add only as much broth at one time as the rice can absorb.) Add the wine and continue stirring. It should be creamy and tender but still firm in the center to the bite. Cooking time should be between 20 and 25 minutes. Stir constantly during the final 5 minutes of cooking.

⊘ Add the remaining 2 tablespoons of butter and the cheese to the cooked rice. Serve immediately.

RISI BISI (RICE AND PEAS)

This is a classic Venetian dish made with fresh peas, but since peas are in season only for a short amount of time, you can substitute frozen peas. Do not substitute the petit pois *or small pea. Use the regular-sized pea for this dish. Carnaroli is our favorite brand of Arborio rice.*

MAKES 4 SERVINGS

3¼ cups chicken broth

2 tablespoons butter

1 tablespoon olive oil

2 ounces pancetta or bacon, diced

1 small yellow onion, finely diced

1 cup short-grain rice (such as Italian arborio)

8 ounces peas, shelled or frozen, thawed

2 tablespoons finely chopped parsley

1 tablespoon fresh lemon juice

2 tablespoons grated Parmesan cheese

Salt and pepper to taste

In a small saucepan bring the chicken broth to a boil. Turn down the heat and simmer. Meanwhile, add the butter and the olive oil to a 3½-quart Dutch oven over medium heat. Add the pancetta or bacon and cook until most of the fat has rendered. Add the diced onion and sauté until translucent, about 5 minutes. Add the rice and stir until each grain is well coated with the oil. Add all of the chicken broth at once and stir. Bring to a simmer, uncovered, and cook for 15 minutes, stirring occasionally. Gently stir in the peas and cook 5 minutes longer. Remove from the heat and gently stir in the parsley, lemon juice, and Parmesan cheese. Season with salt and pepper to taste and serve in warm bowls or alongside meat or fish.

LAQUA FAMILY SLOW-COOKED BEANS

This is a favorite recipe of our good friend chef Randi Laqua's mother, who generously shared it with us. These beans have a wonderful sweet and smoky flavor from the brown sugar and the ham hock, and taste great with barbecued ribs or chicken.

MAKES 8 TO 10 SERVINGS

1 pound (2 cups) Great Northern beans

8 cups water

4 celery stalks, cut in half

2 chicken bouillon cubes

2 bay leaves

1 clove garlic, minced

1 teaspoon ground cloves

¼ teaspoon ground ginger

2 tablespoons dark brown sugar

2 cups chopped yellow onions

2 tablespoons Dijon mustard

1 cup diced canned tomatoes, drained

¾ cup tomato sauce

3 tablespoons tomato paste

1½ pounds ham hock (have the butcher cut into 4 pieces)

- Soak the beans overnight in water in a 5½-quart Dutch oven. Drain the next day. Add 6 cups of the water to cook. In a small saucepan, boil the celery stalks in the remaining 2 cups water until tender. Discard the celery stalks. Pour 1 cup of the celery liquid into a small bowl. Add the chicken bouillon cubes, bay leaves, garlic, cloves, ginger, brown sugar, onions, and mustard. Pour this mixture into the pot with the beans. Cook for 40 minutes over medium-low heat. Add the tomatoes, tomato sauce, tomato paste, and ham hocks and bake until tender for 1½ hours. Serve warm.

TRINITY ALPS BAKED BEANS

This is an indoor or outdoor Dutch oven favorite. Serve in the summertime with grilled sausages or in the winter with baked ham after a long day of skiing. In October we have our annual harvest moon party and we serve only three things: these baked beans, grilled bratwurst on buns, and apple crisp for dessert. Of course, ice cold beer is also available!

MAKES 12 SERVINGS

I pound bacon, cut into ½-inch-thick slices

I pound lean ground beef

I cup finely chopped yellow onion

Two 28-ounce cans baked beans (we like B&M brand)

Two 16-ounce cans kidney beans, drained

Two 16-ounce cans butter beans, drained

I cup brown sugar

I cup ketchup

I½ teaspoons dry mustard

⊘ Preheat the oven to 350° F.

⊘ In a 10- or 12-inch skillet cook the bacon slices over medium heat until slightly crisp. Remove the bacon to a paper towel–lined plate to drain. In another skillet cook the ground beef over medium heat. Break up the beef into smaller pieces with a wooden spoon while it browns. Drain and reserve.

⊘ Put the bacon, ground beef, onions, and beans in a 5½-quart Dutch oven. Mix in the brown sugar, ketchup, and dry mustard. Cover, transfer to the oven, and bake for 1 hour. Reduce the heat to 200° F and bake uncovered for 30 minutes longer. Serve warm.

BAY BRAISED ARTICHOKES

Braising artichokes instead of boiling or steaming them imparts the flavor of the bay and keeps this thistle from getting soggy. The olive oil keeps the artichoke leaves from drying out and adds a nice sheen.

MAKES 4 TO 8 SERVINGS

4 large artichokes

2 cups water

¼ cup extra-virgin olive oil

½ teaspoon salt

2 bay leaves

⟳ Trim the artichoke stems, leaving ½ inch on the artichoke. Cut 1 inch off the top of the leaves. Place the artichokes stem side down in a 5½-quart Dutch oven. Pour in the water, then the olive oil. Add the salt and bay leaves.

⟳ Wrap the lid with a kitchen towel, then put the lid on the pot. Cook over low heat for 50 minutes. Serve warm with melted butter or cold with mayonnaise mixed with fresh lemon juice to taste.

TRICOLOR STUFFED PEPPERS WITH SAUSAGE

We love using the red, yellow, and orange bell peppers in this recipe. The peppers maintain their beautiful color and impart a sweet flavor that blends well with the sausage. This dish is good served warm or at room temperature.

MAKES 6 SERVINGS

6 medium red, yellow, and orange bell peppers (2 of each color)

1 pound bulk Italian sausage

3 cups cooked white rice

3 Roma tomatoes, diced

½ cup freshly grated Parmesan cheese

¼ cup chopped fresh basil

Salt and pepper to taste

2 tablespoons extra-virgin olive oil

⊘ Preheat the oven to 375° F. Cut the tops off the peppers about ½ inch down from the stem and set aside. Remove the seeds from inside the peppers.

⊘ In a 10- or 12-inch skillet brown the sausage over medium heat and break into small pieces with a wooden spoon. Remove the sausage with a slotted spoon and reserve to a paper towel–lined plate.

⊘ In a large bowl mix the cooked rice, sausage, tomatoes, Parmesan, and basil. Season with salt and pepper. Spoon the rice mixture into the peppers, drizzle each with a teaspoon of olive oil, then replace the pepper tops.

⊘ Set a small, round stainless steel cake rack or steamer (opened up) in the bottom of a 5½-quart Dutch oven. Add 1 cup of water. Place the peppers on the rack inside the Dutch oven. Cover the pot, transfer to the oven, and roast for 30 minutes. Remove from the oven and serve.

BRAISED GREENS WITH SMOKED SAUSAGE

The smokiness of the sausage with the greens and a hint of orange make this dish so flavorful. This is a nice side dish to serve with slow-cooked meats, or shrimp and grits. The greens are done when they turn from a vibrant green to an olive green.

MAKES 6 TO 8 SERVINGS

 2 tablespoons olive oil

 4 ounces smoked sausage, cut into ½-inch-long slices

 2 bunches collard greens

 I cup water

 I cup chicken broth

 ½ cup fresh-squeezed orange juice

 I teaspoon grated orange zest

 I tablespoon Worcestershire sauce

 3 tablespoons apple cider vinegar

 Salt and pepper to taste

 Pinch of grated nutmeg

⊘ Put a 5½-quart Dutch oven over medium-low heat and add the olive oil. Add the sausage and cook until golden brown. Remove to a paper towel–lined plate to drain.

⊘ Prepare the collard greens by folding each bunch in half and cutting out the stem. Rinse well, pat dry, and cut into 2-inch-wide strips. Add the greens to the pot, giving a quick toss. Pour in the water, chicken broth, and orange juice.

⊘ Cook the greens down with the lid off for 5 minutes, tossing once or twice. Add the orange zest, Worcestershire sauce, and apple cider vinegar. Cover and cook over low heat for 30 to 35 minutes, or until the greens have all changed to an olive green color.

⊘ Put a strainer in the sink and drain the greens. Transfer them to a medium-sized bowl. Add the cooked sausage, salt, pepper, and nutmeg and toss. Serve from a warm, shallow bowl.

SWEET AND SOUR BRAISED RED CABBAGE

This is a traditional accompaniment to sauerbraten or roast pork. We like to serve it with our Thanksgiving dinner. The cabbage keeps its texture and the caraway seeds add a slight licorice flavor. The enameled Dutch oven prevents the cabbage from discoloring.

MAKES 8 SERVINGS

½ cup red wine vinegar

¼ cup brown sugar

I cup chicken broth

I head red cabbage, outer leaves removed, then quartered, cored, and shredded

I Granny Smith apple, peeled, cored, and chopped

I teaspoon caraway seeds

⊙ Put the red wine vinegar, brown sugar, broth, cabbage, apple, and caraway seeds in a 5½-quart Dutch oven. Mix gently. Place the lid on the pot. Simmer the mixture over low heat for 45 minutes. Serve warm.

COLCANNON

Serve this Irish one-pot dish on St. Patrick's Day with slow-roasted corned beef (see the recipe for Market House Corned Beef on page 101). "Colcannon" comes from the Gaelic word for white winter cabbage. Be sure to serve with crusty rye bread and sweet butter, and don't forget the Guinness.

MAKES 6 SERVINGS

4 tablespoons butter (½ stick)

2 leeks, well cleaned and cut into thin slices (tender white and light green parts only)

½ head cabbage, cut into thin slices

6 medium Yukon Gold potatoes (about 2 pounds), peeled and cubed

1 cup heavy cream

Salt and pepper to taste

¼ cup chopped parsley

৩ Melt the butter in a 5½-quart Dutch oven over medium-low heat. Add the leeks and cook, stirring occasionally, for 5 minutes. Add the cabbage and stir to mix well with the butter and leeks. Simmer the leek-cabbage mixture uncovered over low heat for 15 minutes.

৩ Meanwhile, in a medium-sized saucepan, cover the potatoes with cold water and cook over high heat. When the water begins to boil, turn the heat down to medium. Cook until fork-tender, for about 10 minutes. Drain well and add the potatoes to the cabbage and leeks. Mash with a potato masher. Add the cream and simmer uncovered over low heat for 15 minutes. Season with salt and pepper and serve warm. Sprinkle with chopped parsley for added color and flavor.

MAIN DISHES

Kalua Pork
Pork Loin Braised in Milk
Easy Cassoulet
Moroccan Chicken and Pastina Bake
Country Captain Chicken
Roasted Chicken with Figs, Olives, and Onions
Smoked Sausage, Chicken, and Shrimp Gumbo
Calcutta Chicken Curry
Smothered Chicken with Mushrooms
Slow-Roasted Pheasant with Polenta
Baked Spiced Lamb Shanks
Lamb with Lemon, Oranges, and Green Olives
Baked Daube Provençal
Slow-Roasted Melting Pot Roast
Baked Flank Steak with Spinach, Gorgonzola, and Sun-Dried Tomatoes
Baked Short Ribs with Pasilla Pepper Sauce
Beef Stew with Parsley Dumplings
Market House Corned Beef with Sweet and Sour Sauerkraut Slaw
Braised Tender Beef with Red and Yellow Peppers
Rouladen (Beef Rolls)
Slow-Cooked Beef Short Ribs
Shepherd's Pie
Roasted Mussels with Pinot Grigio
Skimpy Shrimp
Bonnie's Fish Stew

This chapter features our favorite one-pot meals, many of which involve using the Dutch oven for braising. We like to brown the meat first in our cast iron skillet, then transfer it to a large Dutch oven, add the liquid suggested in the recipe, and cover and cook for several hours. Braising is ideal for cooking the tough muscle cuts of meat, such as chuck roast, short ribs, shanks, shoulder meat, and stew meat. Using the Dutch oven for slow cooking in the oven results in evenly cooked entreés that are fork tender—no knives are needed!

The beauty of one-pot meals is that they can be easy centerpieces of a Sunday supper. Served with crusty bread, a simple green salad, and a favorite dessert, they allow you to enjoy family and friends without being busy with last-minute preparations in the kitchen. Delicious aromas will greet your guests, and you can be a very relaxed host. As the seasons change, these dishes are a welcome diversion from the outdoor grill. We love to serve the Baked Short Ribs with Pasilla Pepper Sauce or the Braised Tender Beef with Red and Yellow Peppers on a cool Northwest evening.

There is a very friendly, communal sharing that is present with one-pot meals, and recipes from around the world celebrate slow cooking. In Provence, the *daube*—a traditional meat stew often made with lamb—has a special pot that is set inside the hearth of a wood-burning fireplace and allowed to cook for hours while the flavors blend and the meat becomes tender. We hope you enjoy these recipes and develop many of your own.

KALUA PORK

Traditionally cooked outdoors in a special pit, this Hawaiian specialty can be slow-cooked in a Dutch oven for 5 hours. The shredded meat makes delicious sandwiches with a little of your favorite barbecue sauce added. A special thanks to the Lees and the Changs of Kaneohe, Hawaii, for sharing this recipe with us. Pulled pork sandwiches are a big hit with all ages.

MAKES 8 TO 10 SERVINGS

   5 pounds boneless pork butt roast, rolled

   4 to 6 cups water

   1 tablespoon hickory seasoning liquid smoke

   2 tablespoons coarse Hawaiian salt (white) or sea salt

   2 cups of your favorite barbecue sauce

꙳ Preheat the oven to 350° F.

꙳ Put the pork roast in a 5½-quart Dutch oven. Add enough water to surround the roast half of the way up, leaving half of the roast out of the water. Add the liquid smoke and salt to the water. Cover and bake for 3 hours. Turn the oven down to 250° F and continue to bake for 2 hours longer, for a total of 5 hours. Remove from the oven, leave the cover on, and let cool slightly.

꙳ Remove the strings. Shred the meat with two forks, discarding the fat. You can add some of the barbecue sauce and serve on toasted buns. We like to serve these delicious sandwiches with coleslaw.

Note: You can shred the cooked meat and freeze it for future use.

PORK LOIN BRAISED IN MILK

In Guiliano Hazan's cookbook How to Cook Italian, *he shares his family recipe for pan-roasting the pork with milk. This technique produces a very tender and moist roast, and the milk and juices create a delicious sauce.*

MAKES 6 SERVINGS

I tablespoon butter
2 tablespoons vegetable oil
2 pounds pork loin
Salt and freshly ground black pepper to taste
2½ cups whole milk

⊙ Put the butter and oil in a 3 ½-quart Dutch oven over medium heat. Brown the meat evenly on all sides. Season the pork with salt and pepper and add I cup of the milk. Turn the heat down to low, and cover the pot. Cook for 20 minutes, turning several times. Add the remaining milk and continue cooking, turning the meat every 20 minutes. The roast is done in a total of I½ hours, or when it is fork tender.

⊙ Remove the pork loin from the pan and cut into thin slices. Return to the sauce that formed in the pan, heat, and serve right away.

EASY CASSOULET

There are many different recipes for cassoulet, but this one is simple and flavorful. Serve it as a main course or as a side dish. The ingredients list is long, but the final dish is full of delicious flavors. The bread crumbs add a crisp texture to the soft beans.

MAKES 8 SERVINGS

2 cups dried navy beans, rinsed and picked over

2 medium yellow onions, chopped

1 bouquet garni (8 parsley sprigs, 3 peeled garlic cloves, 6 sprigs fresh thyme, 4 whole cloves, and 2 bay leaves tied in cheesecloth)

2 cups chicken broth

½ cup dry red wine

½ cup brandy

½ cup canned crushed tomatoes

3 tablespoons tomato paste

1 pound smoked Polish sausage, cut into ¼-inch-thick slices

1 pound smoked chicken or duck sausage, cut into ¼-inch-thick slices

1 Granny Smith apple, peeled and cut into ½-inch-thick slices

8 ounces bacon, cut into ¼-inch-thick slices

2 cups fresh breadcrumbs

3 tablespoons butter, melted

½ cup coarsely chopped fresh parsley

◯ Preheat the oven to 400° F.

◯ In a large, heavy saucepan bring 8 cups of water to a boil. Add the navy beans and cook for 1 minute. Remove from the heat and let stand, covered, for 1 hour. Add the onions and the bouquet garni to the beans and bring to a boil over high heat. Turn down the heat to low and simmer for 1 hour. Drain the beans and discard the bouquet garni.

In a large Dutch oven bring the chicken broth, red wine, brandy, and tomatoes to a boil. Stir in the tomato paste. Add the Polish sausage, the smoked chicken or duck sausage, and the apple and stir to mix well. Heat a skillet over medium heat and add the bacon, crisping for about 3 minutes on each side. Remove to a cutting board and cut into ½-inch pieces; set aside.

In a medium-sized bowl toss the breadcrumbs with the melted better and parsley. Sprinkle the breadcrumbs and bacon evenly over the top of the casserole. Transfer to the oven and bake uncovered for 30 minutes. Turn down the heat to 350° F and bake for 1 hour longer, or until the beans are cooked but still a bit firm. Serve in warm bowls with a nice crisp salad.

MOROCCAN CHICKEN AND PASTINA BAKE

Eating pasta this way can become very addicting. The pasta absorbs all of the flavors of the chicken broth and the sweetness of the roasted red onions and tomatoes. It's hard to believe that pasta can cook successfully this way, but it works and it's easy.

MAKES 6 SERVINGS

1 pound cherry tomatoes, rinsed and stemmed

2 tablespoons olive oil

1 teaspoon salt, plus more to taste

1 teaspoon pepper, plus more to taste

10 chicken thighs (skinless)

10 cloves garlic, peeled and left whole

1 large red onion, peeled, halved, and cut into thin slices

2 cups chicken broth

2 cups small dried pasta shells or penne

2 cinnamon sticks, halved lengthwise

Zest and juice of 1 orange

◌ Preheat the oven to 400° F.

◌ Add the cherry tomatoes to a 5½-quart Dutch oven. Toss with the olive oil, salt, and pepper. Put in the oven and bake for 15 minutes.

◌ Remove from the oven and add the chicken thighs, garlic cloves, and red onions. Lightly salt and pepper the dish. Add the chicken broth and pasta. Push down the pasta a few times during cooking with the back of a spatula to make sure it is submerged. Add the cinnamon sticks, orange zest, and orange juice. Return the pot to the oven and bake uncovered for 40 to 45 minutes, or until the pasta is tender and the chicken is cooked. Add salt and pepper to taste.

COUNTRY CAPTAIN CHICKEN

Our friend Marion Cunningham is one of our favorite cookbook authors.
(Everything she cooks tastes so good!) This is an easy version of one of her
favorite recipes. The Madras curry powder is a blend of spices that gives
this dish its characteristic flavor.

MAKES 4 TO 6 SERVINGS

4 tablespoons butter (½ stick)

2 tablespoons vegetable oil

¼ cup all-purpose flour, seasoned with 1 teaspoon salt and ¼ teaspoon
    pepper, for coating

4 chicken breasts (boneless and skinless), cut into 1-inch strips

1 medium yellow onion, chopped

1 Granny Smith apple, peeled, cored, and chopped

3 cloves garlic, peeled and chopped

1 tablespoon Madras curry powder

One 14.5-ounce can diced tomatoes, drained

1 cup chicken broth

¼ cup dried currants

2 cups jasmine rice

4 cups water

Chunky Mango Chutney (see recipe on page 122), for garnish

Toasted unsweetened coconut, for garnish

❧ Put a 5½-quart Dutch oven over medium heat. Add the butter and vegetable oil. Coat the chicken strips with the seasoned flour. Lightly brown the
chicken strips. Remove and set aside. Turn the heat down to low. Add the
onions, apple, and garlic. Cook for 10 minutes. Mix in the curry and stir for
1 minute. Add the tomatoes, chicken broth, and currants. Simmer uncovered
over low heat for 20 minutes. Add the chicken and cook 10 minutes longer.
Meanwhile, cook the rice in the water for 25 minutes.

❧ Spoon over the cooked rice and top with the mango chutney and coconut.

ROASTED CHICKEN WITH FIGS, OLIVES, AND ONIONS

We love the flavor of this chicken dish. The saltiness of the olives complements the sweetness of the figs. It's always fun to see which member of the family likes which part of the chicken. The kids almost always want the drumsticks.

MAKES 4 SERVINGS

One 3- to 3½-pound young fryer chicken

6 tablespoons olive oil

2 tablespoons butter, softened

2 teaspoons kosher salt

1 teaspoon freshly cracked pepper

2 teaspoons dried herbes de Provence

1 teaspoon ground fennel seeds

1 medium yellow onion, halved and coarsely chopped

½ cup halved kalamata olives

8 figs, stemmed and halved

Sauce

½ cup dry white wine

3 tablespoons Madeira

2 cups chicken broth

1 tablespoon butter

2 tablespoons all-purpose flour

⊙ Move the racks to the bottom of the oven. Preheat the oven to 425° F.

⊙ Remove the neck, gizzards, and any other chicken parts from inside the cavity of the chicken. Rinse well with cold water inside and out and pat dry. Place on a cutting board and rub with half of the olive oil. Slip the butter between the breast meat and the skin of the chicken. Rub the salt, pepper, herbes de Provence, and ground fennel seeds all over the chicken.

- Pour the remaining olive oil in a 5½-quart Dutch oven. Add the onions and place the chicken, breast side up, on top of the onions. Scatter the olives and the figs around the chicken and put it into the preheated oven.

- Roast for 30 minutes uncovered. Baste the chicken with its own juices every 20 minutes. Turn the heat down to 350° F and roast for 40 minutes longer (or until the temperature behind the leg joint reads 160° F and the juices run clear when the skin is cut behind the chicken's back leg). Remove the chicken to a platter with the figs, olives, and onions, making sure to leave the juice in the pot.

- To make the sauce, heat the pot over medium heat and deglaze the pan with the white wine and Madeira, scraping up any browned bits. Add the chicken broth and turn the heat to medium-high. Reduce by half. Turn the heat down to medium-low.

- In a small bowl add the butter to the flour and knead together with your fingers until combined into a paste. Add 1 tablespoon of the flour and butter mixture to the sauce, whisking continuously until incorporated and the sauce starts to thicken. If you want the sauce a little thicker, add another tablespoon of the flour and butter mixture. Pour the sauce into a small gravy boat and serve alongside the chicken, or carve the chicken and return it to the platter with the figs, olives, and onions. Pour the sauce over the meat and serve.

SMOKED SAUSAGE, CHICKEN, AND SHRIMP GUMBO

This is a delicious one-pot dish. You can chop the vegetables a day ahead; then it's less work on the day you're entertaining. Serve in shallow bowls with a mound of steamed rice in the center and a sprinkle of gumbo file powder (sassafras), chopped parsley, and green onions over the top. We like to sauté the prawns in butter and add them at the very end.

MAKES 8 SERVINGS

1 rotisserie chicken

¼ cup olive oil

2½ cups chopped yellow onion

4 cloves garlic, peeled and chopped

1 cup chopped green bell pepper

1 cup chopped red bell pepper

1 tablespoon Hungarian paprika

½ cup butter (1 stick), cut into pieces, plus 1 tablespoon extra for sautéing prawns

½ cup all-purpose flour

One 28-ounce can diced tomatoes with juice (we prefer fire-roasted tomatoes)

2½ cups chicken broth

1 tablespoon Old Bay seasoning

1 tablespoon chili powder

Pinch of cayenne

1 pound smoked andouille sausage, cut into ½-inch slices

8 ounces large prawns, shelled and deveined

Steamed jasmine rice

Chopped green onion, for garnish

Chopped parsley, for garnish

Gumbo file powder, for garnish

Tabasco sauce, for serving (optional)

◌ Remove the skin and bones from the chicken. Cut the meat into 1-inch pieces and reserve until ready to add.

◌ Heat the olive oil in a 5½-quart Dutch oven over medium heat. Add the onion, garlic, peppers, and paprika and cook for several minutes. Remove and reserve in a bowl.

◌ Scrape up any brown particles, then turn down the heat to medium-low. Melt the butter pieces. Blend in the flour to create a roux. Stirring continuously with a heat-proof spatula, cook the roux for 10 minutes until it is the color of peanut butter. Stir in the cooked onion, peppers, and garlic. Add the tomatoes with their juice and the chicken broth. Stir until the mixture thickens.

◌ Add the Old Bay seasoning, andouille sausage, and cooked chicken pieces. Simmer uncovered over low heat for 15 minutes. Sauté the prawns in the remaining tablespoon of butter until they turn pink, and add to the finished gumbo. Serve with jasmine rice and sprinkle with green onion, parsley, and a dash of file powder. (Serve with Tabasco at the table.)

Notes: Using butter to make the roux is much easier than using oil; the butter and flour combine better and the butter adds a nice nutty flavor. Also, if you can't find fire-roasted diced tomatoes, regular diced tomatoes with juice will work fine.

CALCUTTA CHICKEN CURRY

Just a few ingredients and a variety of condiments bring this chicken curry to the table. Serve with steamed rice. This is based on one of our favorite dishes served at the original Trader Vic's restaurant in Seattle.

MAKES 6 SERVINGS

I teaspoon salt

¼ teaspoon pepper

½ cup flour

2 pounds chicken breasts (boneless and skinless), cut into ½-inch strips

4 tablespoons butter (½ stick)

2 tablespoons vegetable oil

1½ cups finely chopped yellow onion

1½ cups peeled and finely chopped carrot

½ cup finely chopped celery

3 tablespoons Madras curry powder

I teaspoon ground turmeric

One 14.5-ounce can unsweetened coconut milk

1½ cups chicken broth

One 14.5-ounce can diced tomatoes, drained

Garnishes

Chunky Mango Chutney (see recipe on page 122)

I red apple, diced

Dried currants

Sweetened shredded coconut

I cup chopped salted cashews mixed with ¼ cup chopped crystallized ginger

Lime wedges

↪ Mix the salt, pepper, and flour together in a bowl and add the chicken pieces to coat.

↪ Heat 2 tablespoons of the butter and 1 tablespoon of the oil over medium heat in a large Dutch oven. Add the chicken in two batches, sautéing each batch until lightly browned; remove the chicken to a plate. Add the remaining butter and oil to the warm pot, and add the onions, carrots, and celery. Cook uncovered for 5 minutes, stirring often. Add the curry powder and turmeric and cook for 1 minute. Add the coconut milk, chicken broth, and tomatoes and stir. Turn the heat down, partially cover the pot, and cook for 20 minutes. Remove the lid and gently cook for 10 minutes, or until the sauce thickens slightly. Serve with steamed rice and garnishes.

SMOTHERED CHICKEN
WITH MUSHROOMS

A Sunday favorite! Easy to prepare, then just put in the oven and bake. It's also delicious reheated the next day.

MAKES 6 SERVINGS

4 tablespoons butter (½ stick)

8 ounces mushrooms, cut into thin slices (see note)

3 chicken breast halves (boneless and skinless), cut in half crosswise

3 chicken thighs (boneless and skinless), cut in half crosswise

¼ cup all-purpose flour, seasoned with salt and pepper, for coating

2 tablespoons vegetable oil

1 yellow onion, sliced

1 cup heavy cream

2 tablespoons dry sherry

↺ Preheat the oven to 350° F.

↺ Melt 2 tablespoons of the butter in a 5½-quart Dutch oven over medium heat. Sauté the mushrooms briefly and then transfer to a plate and reserve. Coat the chicken pieces with the seasoned flour. Add the remaining butter and the vegetable oil to the Dutch oven and brown the chicken pieces on both sides in batches. Spoon off the excess fat. Add the chicken back into the pot. Scatter the mushrooms and onions over the chicken pieces in the Dutch oven. Pour the cream and sherry over the chicken. Place a piece of buttered parchment paper on top of the chicken, cover with the lid, and bake for 50 minutes.

↺ Remove from the oven and serve with buttered noodles or rice and spring asparagus.

Note: Fresh morel mushrooms are wonderful in this recipe; be sure to rinse them well before using.

SLOW-ROASTED PHEASANT WITH POLENTA

If you are fortunate to have a hunter in your family, you can enjoy the bounty of a successful hunt. If not, you can order pheasant through a specialty meat market (see Resources, page 141). The slow baking makes the pheasant fall off the bone.

MAKES 8 SERVINGS

 2 tablespoons olive oil

 10 tablespoons butter (1¼ sticks)

 2 pheasants, cut into pieces and lightly floured

 1 quart (4 cups) red wine

 ¼ cup all-purpose flour

 1 tablespoon sugar

 1 large sweet yellow onion, peeled, halved, and cut into thin slices

 1-2-3 Polenta (see recipe on page 53)

⊘ Preheat the oven to 350° F.

⊘ In a 5½-quart Dutch oven over medium heat, heat the olive oil and 2 tablespoons of the butter together and sauté the floured pheasant pieces until browned all over. Add more oil and butter if necessary. Transfer to a platter.

⊘ Pour the red wine into the pot and bring to a boil. Boil for 5 minutes. Turn down the heat, and mix another 4 tablespoons of the butter and the flour together until well blended. Stir into the boiling wine in small pieces, stirring to thicken and form a sauce. Pour the red wine sauce into a medium-sized bowl. Put the pheasant back into the pot and pour the sauce over the pheasant. Place a piece of parchment paper directly on top. Cover with the lid slightly ajar. Transfer to the oven and bake for 1 hour.

⊘ Meanwhile, melt the remaining butter (4 tablespoons) in a small skillet, and add the sugar and onions. Cook the onions over low heat until soft. Add to the pheasant after it has been baking for 30 minutes. Re-cover with parchment paper and continue baking for 45 minutes.

⊘ Serve the pheasant with the polenta and a crisp, green salad.

BAKED SPICED LAMB SHANKS

The spices give a nice flavor to the lamb and make it less gamey tasting. We love this dish served with Israeli couscous and a tzatziki sauce on the side. The lamb just falls off the bone.

MAKES 6 TO 8 SERVINGS

Rub

1½ teaspoons mustard seeds

1½ teaspoons fennel seeds

1½ teaspoons coriander seeds

1 teaspoon cumin seeds

¼ teaspoon smoked paprika

½ teaspoon salt

Lamb Shanks

6 pounds lamb shanks, lightly seasoned with salt and pepper

2 tablespoons peeled and chopped garlic

¼ cup olive oil

2 medium yellow onions, peeled and cut into thin slices

2 cups Muir Glen fire-roasted tomatoes or canned diced tomatoes, with their juices

3 cups homemade or low-sodium chicken broth

⊘ For the rub, blend the mustard, fennel, coriander, and cumin seeds in a spice or coffee grinder. Shake into a small bowl. Add the paprika and salt and mix with a fork to combine.

⊘ For the lamb, rub the shanks all over with half the garlic, then rub with the spice mixture listed above. Heat 3 tablespoons of the olive oil in a 5½-quart Dutch oven over medium heat. Add the lamb shanks and brown on all sides for about 3 minutes per side. Remove to a plate.

ᴐ Add the remaining tablespoon of olive oil and sauté the yellow onions until soft, for about 5 minutes. Add the remaining garlic and sauté for 1 minute longer. Add the tomatoes and chicken broth and bring to a boil over medium-high heat. Turn off the heat and add the lamb shanks. Place in the oven on the middle rack and cook with the lid on for 1 hour. Remove the lid and bake for 30 minutes more. Remove from the oven and serve with Israeli couscous.

LAMB WITH LEMON, ORANGES, AND GREEN OLIVES

This melt-in-your-mouth meat dish is delicious served over couscous. We use Near East original couscous that cooks in 5 minutes. Fresh spinach tossed with toasted pine nuts, olive oil, and lemon juice completes the meal. We prefer to cut the lamb into pieces.

MAKES 6 SERVINGS

6 tablespoons olive oil

3½ pounds leg of lamb (boneless), trimmed and cut into 2-inch chunks

Salt and pepper to taste

2 cups chopped yellow onion

3 cloves garlic, peeled and left whole

Two 14.5-ounce cans tomato sauce

2 cups red wine

I teaspoon garam masala (see Resources, page I4I)

¼ cup dried currants

½ lemon, cut into thin slices

½ orange, cut into thin slices

8 to IO large pitted green olives

I cinnamon stick

☙ Preheat the oven to 350° F.

☙ Heat 2 tablespoons of the olive oil over medium-high heat in a large Dutch oven. Season the chunks of meat with salt and pepper. Add a third of the meat to the pot and brown on both sides. Remove the meat to a platter with a slotted spoon and reserve. Repeat this cycle two more times until all of the meat is browned and reserved.

∂ Add the onions to the drippings in the pan and sauté briefly. Add the garlic and all of the meat to the Dutch oven. Pour in the tomato sauce, wine, and garam masala. Sprinkle the currants over everything. Add the lemon, orange, green olives, and cinnamon stick. With a large spoon gently stir all of the ingredients together, coating the meat with the sauce. Wrap the lid of the Dutch oven with a kitchen towel and place on top of the pot.

∂ Transfer to the oven and bake in the center for 2 hours. Serve right away with couscous or oven-baked potatoes tossed with fresh herbs.

BAKED DAUBE PROVENÇAL

A specialty from the Provence region of France, this is one of the most flavorful oven-baked beef (or lamb) stews, with tender meat and a delicious sauce, cooked for two hours. Serve with small boiled whole potatoes and a simple Bibb lettuce salad with Dijon dressing.

MAKES 6 SERVINGS

2½ to 3 pounds beef chuck roast

¼ cup all-purpose flour, seasoned with salt and pepper, for coating

3 tablespoons olive oil

2 strips bacon, cut crosswise into 1-inch slices

1 medium sweet yellow onion, cut into crescent slices

1 standard bottle red wine

¼ cup tomato paste

2 bay leaves

2 strips of orange zest

One 14.5-ounce can chopped tomatoes, drained

⊘ Preheat the oven to 325° F.

⊘ Trim the fat from the beef and cut into 2-inch pieces. Put the seasoned flour in a medium-sized bowl and coat the pieces of meat with the flour mixture.

⊘ Heat the olive oil over medium heat in a 5½-quart Dutch oven. Brown the meat in two batches and remove to a platter, with the juices. Add the bacon and onions and cook for 3 to 4 minutes. Pour in the red wine and simmer for 5 minutes. Add the tomato paste, bay leaves, and orange zest. Stir and simmer for 5 minutes. Add the browned meat and juices back into the pot.

⊘ Place a piece of buttered parchment paper directly on top of the meat, cover and put in the preheated oven. Bake for 1½ hours. Remove from the oven and discard the parchment paper. Add the chopped tomatoes and bake uncovered for an additional 30 minutes.

SLOW-ROASTED MELTING POT ROAST

The flavor of a beef chuck roast is a winter Sunday dinner favorite. A change from summer grilled meats, this roast is very tender and flavorful. Serve with boiled, lightly mashed, buttered potatoes and a horseradish–sour cream sauce. If there is any meat left over, it makes a great sandwich: Coarsely chop the cold roast in a food processor and mix it with onions and mayonnaise.

MAKES 6 SERVINGS

2 tablespoons vegetable oil

2½ pounds beef chuck pot roast, trimmed and patted dry

Salt and pepper to taste

1 large yellow onion, peeled, halved, and cut into thin slices

3 large cloves garlic, peeled

1 cup water

½ cup heavy cream

⊘ Preheat the oven to 350° F.

⊘ In a 5½-quart Dutch oven add the oil and heat over medium heat. Sear the meat on all sides. Sprinkle with salt and pepper. Add the onions, garlic cloves, and water. Cover and bake for 2 hours. Remove the roast and add the cream to the onions and pan juices, and cook for 2 minutes. Spoon the sauce over the sliced roast.

Roasting

I t is important to differentiate Dutch oven roasting from dry roasting. Dry roasting takes place in a shallower pan at high temperatures. Dutch oven roasting results in extra moisture in the pot because of its higher sides. We recommend roasting in the Dutch oven when the recipe calls for any kind of liquid and is slow-cooked at a moderate temperature.

BAKED FLANK STEAK WITH SPINACH, GORGONZOLA, AND SUN-DRIED TOMATOES

This dish is simple and delicious. Searing the meat keeps the juices in, and during the cooking the Gorgonzola melts into the sauce. Try to find Muir Glen fire-roasted tomatoes—we love their flavor and smokiness.

MAKES 4 SERVINGS

1½ pounds flank steak

1½ cups spinach, washed and drained

¼ cup sun-dried tomatoes, packed in oil and drained

½ cup Gorgonzola cheese, crumbled

¼ cup all-purpose flour, seasoned with salt and pepper, for coating

3 tablespoons olive oil

2 cups red wine

One 14.5-ounce can Muir Glen fire-roasted whole tomatoes, drained

⊘ Preheat the oven to 350° F.

⊘ Lay the flank steak flat. Trim the narrow end so the length of the steak is about 8 inches. Arrange the spinach lengthwise down the steak. Sprinkle the sun-dried tomatoes down the center of the spinach. Top with the Gorgonzola cheese in one continuous strip. Close the sides of the steak together and make a tie four times with butcher string 2 inches apart. Roll the flank steak in the seasoned flour to lightly coat.

⊘ Heat the olive oil in a 5½-quart Dutch oven over medium heat. When the oil is hot, add the flank steak and brown on all sides. Add the red wine and let simmer for several minutes, then add the tomatoes. Transfer to the oven and bake covered for 1 hour. Let rest for 10 minutes before slicing. Serve with oven-roasted potatoes.

BAKED SHORT RIBS WITH PASILLA PEPPER SAUCE

The pasilla pepper is one of our favorite peppers to cook with. It is wonderful in moles and sauces. One of the "holy trinity" of peppers, pasilla is a dried chilaca chile, also known as chile negro. *This smoky yet mild pepper gives this dish depth of flavor.*

MAKES 6 TO 8 SERVINGS

I dried pasilla pepper, rehydrated, seeded, stemmed, and finely chopped

4 pounds beef short ribs (boneless), rinsed and patted dry, excess fat trimmed

Salt and freshly ground black pepper

I tablespoon olive oil

I tablespoon butter

I medium yellow onion, diced

4 cloves garlic, peeled and minced

½ cup puréed roasted red peppers (if using canned roasted red peppers, be sure to drain and rinse them before puréeing)

One 14.5-ounce can tomato sauce

½ cup red wine

2 whole star anise

¼ teaspoon ground cinnamon

I teaspoon Chinese five-spice powder

2 bay leaves

⊘ Position a rack in the center of the oven and preheat to 350° F. To rehydrate the pasilla pepper, place it in a bowl, cover with boiling hot water, and soak for 5 minutes.

⊘ To prepare the ribs, season with salt and pepper on both sides. Put a 12-inch cast iron skillet over medium-high heat, then add the ribs, fat side down. Cook turning once, until browned on all sides, for 2 to 3 minutes. Transfer the ribs to a plate and reserve.

⊘ Meanwhile, in a 5½-quart Dutch oven add the oil and butter and heat over medium-low heat. Add the onions and cook until they start to soften, for about 5 minutes. Add the garlic and cook for 2 minutes, stirring occasionally. Add the puréed roasted red peppers, pasilla pepper, tomato sauce, red wine, star anise, cinnamon, five-spice powder, and bay leaves. Add the short ribs back to the pot, and wrap the lid with a slightly damp kitchen towel, pulling tight, placing the corners on top of the pot. Do not let the towel fall into the dish.

⊘ Put the Dutch oven in the preheated oven on the middle rack. Cook until the meat falls apart easily with a fork, about 1½ to 2 hours. Serve on a plate with buttered egg noodles.

BEEF STEW WITH PARSLEY DUMPLINGS

This stew is perfect on a cold Northwest evening, and the dumplings soak up some of the delicious sauce. Serve with a nice crisp salad.

MAKES 8 SERVINGS

I cup all-purpose flour, for coating

2½ teaspoons salt

¼ teaspoon pepper

2 pounds beef chuck or round (boneless), trimmed and cut into I- to
1½-inch cubes

2 tablespoons butter

¼ cup olive oil, divided

2 bay leaves

I bouquet garni (see page 76 and note)

1½ teaspoons dried herbes de Provence

½ cup chopped celery tops

2 parsley sprigs

I cup water

I cup red wine

I cup beef broth

2 medium yellow onions, peeled and chopped

3 medium carrots, peeled and halved crosswise

4 medium new potatoes, scrubbed and quartered

2 medium (or 4 small) white turnips, peeled, stemmed, and quartered

Stew

☉ Preheat the oven to 350° F.

☉ Spread the flour on a baking sheet lined with wax paper. Salt and pepper
the meat, then roll the beef cubes in the flour, coating all sides and shaking
off any excess.

⊘ Heat the butter and olive oil in a 5½-quart Dutch oven over medium-high heat. Brown the meat in batches, adding more butter if necessary. Turn using tongs to brown on all sides. Do not overcrowd the meat or it will sweat rather than brown. Take out the browned meat and reserve on a large plate.

⊘ Return all browned beef to the Dutch oven, add the bay leaves, bouquet garni, herbes de Provence, thyme, celery tops, and parsley sprigs. Toss to coat with the drippings. Add the water, red wine, and beef broth and bring to a boil. Transfer the pot to the center rack in the oven. With the lid slighly ajar, bake for 2 hours.

⊘ Add the yellow onions, carrots, potatoes, turnips, and celery and bake completly covered for 30 more minutes. Meanwhile, make the dumplings (see ingredients and instructions below).

Parsley Dumplings

1¼ cups all-purpose flour

⅔ cup cornmeal

2½ teaspoons baking powder

½ teaspoon salt

7 tablespoons butter, chilled

2 tablespoons chopped parsley

1 cup whole milk

½ teaspoon kosher salt or sea salt (see Resources, page 141)

Melted butter, for browning (optional)

⊘ Whisk together the flour, cornmeal, baking powder, and salt in a large bowl. Cut the butter into tablespoon-sized pieces. Using a pastry blender or your fingers, work quickly so the butter stays nice and cold. Work the butter into the flour mixture until the pieces are pea-sized. (You can also transfer the flour mixture to a food processor fitted with a steel blade, add the butter, and pulse 5 or 6 times.) Gently mix in the parsley, using your hands. Add the milk and mix gently, just until the ingredients are incorporated.

⊘ Temporarily remove the stew from the oven. Using a large spoon, scoop up some of the dumpling mixture and drop the batter by 10 rounded spoonfuls on top of the stew (on top of the meat or vegetables, not on the liquid, as this makes the dumplings soggy), 2 to 3 inches apart, allowing room for them to expand.

☉ Sprinkle the tops with kosher salt and return to the oven with the lid off. Cook for 20 to 25 minutes, uncovered. If you want to brown the tops of the dumplings more, brush them with melted butter and turn on the broiler for the last few minutes. Serve in bowls with a dumpling or two on top.

Note: As a substitution for the bouquet garni, try using a tea ball filled with 6 juniper berries, two star anise, 2 cardamon pods, and 6 peppercorns.

Baking

Baking stews or roasts in the Dutch oven provides a source of even heat from the top, sides, and bottom of the pot. This allows the flavors to blend and results in a delicious, rich sauce. Be sure to use oven mitts when removing the hot Dutch oven from your oven. It's hot and heavy, and will keep your food nice and warm.

MARKET HOUSE CORNED BEEF WITH SWEET AND SOUR SAUERKRAUT SLAW

Seattleites have a great source for corned beef: Market House Corned Beef from Market House Meats. Serve with parsley-buttered new potatoes and sweet and sour sauerkraut slaw. Use the leftover slaw and corned beef for Reuben sandwiches the next day.

MAKES 6 SERVINGS

Corned Beef

4 to 5 pounds corned beef

☙ Preheat the oven to 350° F. Bake the corned beef in ½ inch of water for 3½ hours, in a covered 5½-quart Dutch oven. Remove the cover and bake for 30 more minutes. Serve at room temperature, thickly sliced with the sauerkraut slaw and an assortment of mustards and horseradish.

Sweet and Sour Sauerkraut Slaw

4 cups sauerkraut, rinsed and well drained
1 cup chopped celery
½ cup chopped red bell pepper
½ cup chopped green bell pepper
1 cup chopped green onions
1 cup sugar
¼ cup vegetable oil
¾ cup white vinegar

☙ Put the sauerkraut, celery, red and green bell peppers, and green onions in a bowl. Mix well. Blend the sugar, vegetable oil, and vinegar together and pour over the salad mix. Cover and refrigerate for several hours before serving.

BRAISED TENDER BEEF WITH
RED AND YELLOW PEPPERS

The flavors of the peppers and carrots in this recipe melt together and produce a wonderful sauce for the tender chunks of beef. Serve with buttered egg noddles and a crisp green salad.

MAKES 6 SERVINGS

2½ to 3 pounds beef chuck roast, trimmed and cut into 2-inch pieces

½ cup all-purpose flour, seasoned with salt and pepper, for coating

3 tablespoons olive oil

I cup chopped yellow onions

3 cloves garlic, peeled and minced

I medium red bell pepper, cut into ½-inch strips

I medium yellow bell pepper, cut into ½-inch strips

2 strips orange zest

3 large carrots, peeled and cut into 2- by ½-inch sticks

¾ cup red wine

One 28-ounce can diced tomatoes in purée

I teaspoon chopped fresh rosemary

½ teaspoon crushed red pepper flakes

I teaspoon fennel seeds, toasted

½ cup chopped fresh parsley, for garnish

❍ Preheat the oven to 350° F. Lightly coat the beef cubes with the seasoned flour. Heat I tablespoon olive oil in a 5½-quart Dutch oven over medium heat. Brown the meat on both sides, remove, and transfer to a plate. Turn down the heat and add the remaining olive oil, onions, and garlic, stirring until soft. Add the peppers and sauté briefly. Add the orange zest, carrots, red wine, tomatoes in purée, rosemary, red pepper flakes, and fennel seeds.

❍ Place a piece of parchment paper directly on top of the meat to prevent excess moisture from dripping back into the dish. Bake for 1½ hours or until the meat is tender. Sprinkle with parsley and serve.

ROULADEN (BEEF ROLLS)

This is a good way to serve round steak for a winter Sunday supper. We like it better than the usual Swiss steak preparation and serve it with spaetzle (buttered egg noodles; see the recipe on page 55) and buttered carrots with toasted caraway seeds.

MAKES 6 SERVINGS

8 thick strips bacon, cut in half

8 slices round steak, pounded to ¼-inch thickness, 4 inches wide and 6 to 8 inches long

Salt and pepper to taste

8 teaspoons Dijon mustard

½ cup finely chopped yellow onion

8 carrot sticks, ½ inch wide by 5 inches long

8 dill pickle spears, ½ inch wide by 5 inches long

½ cup chopped parsley

¼ cup flour, seasoned with salt and pepper, for coating

2 tablespoons vegetable oil

2 tablespoons butter

One 28-ounce can diced tomatoes, with juice

¼ cup French onion soup mix

⊘ Preheat the oven to 350° F.

⊘ In a 10- or 12-inch skillet cook the bacon over medium heat for 4 minutes, turning once. Drain and reserve. Lay the beef slices flat on the counter on a prep surface such as wax paper. Season with salt and pepper. Lightly spread each piece of meat with 1 teaspoon of the Dijon mustard and then sprinkle with 1 tablespoon of the chopped onion. Place two pieces of bacon 1 inch from the end of the meat slice and top with a carrot stick and a pickle spear. Sprinkle each piece of meat with parsley. Carefully roll each rouladen into a tight bundle. Tie each roll twice with butcher string, one tie on each end.

↺ Roll the bundles in the seasoned flour (shaking off any excess flour). Add the vegetable oil and butter to a 5½-quart Dutch oven over medium heat. Place the beef rolls in the pot and brown evenly on all sides.

↺ Pour the diced tomatoes with juice into a small bowl and stir in the French onion soup mix. Pour the mixture into the Dutch oven over the rolls, then place a piece of parchment paper directly on top of the beef rolls. Cover and bake for 1 hour.

SLOW-COOKED BEEF SHORT RIBS

This recipe is easy and flavorful—the meat falls off the bone and melts in your mouth. A good friend made this dish for us many years ago, and it is still a favorite today. Braising in the oven yields a rich, smooth sauce.

MAKES 6 SERVINGS

4 pounds beef short ribs

½ cup all-purpose flour, for coating

I teaspoon salt

½ teaspoon pepper

4 tablespoons butter (½ stick)

2 tablespoons olive oil

2 medium yellow onions, cut into thin slices

2 tablespoons brown sugar

I tablespoon vinegar

½ teaspoon dry mustard

½ cup ketchup

½ cup beer

I cup beef broth

6 medium carrots (about I½ pounds), peeled and halved

⊘ Preheat the oven to 350° F.

⊘ Lightly coat the short ribs in the flour, shaking off excess flour. Sprinkle with salt and pepper. Add the butter and olive oil to a 12-inch skillet and brown several ribs at a time over medium heat (do not crowd the meat or it will stew rather than brown). Remove the ribs to a baking sheet and continue browning the rest of the ribs in batches. Reduce the heat to medium-low, add the onions, and cook until soft, for about 5 minutes.

⊘ In a 5½-quart enameled Dutch oven, add the onions and the browned ribs. Add the brown sugar, vinegar, dry mustard, ketchup, beer, and beef broth. Put it in the oven, covered, for I½ hours. Add the carrots and bake, covered, for I hour longer. Remove from the oven and serve with mashed potatoes or polenta (see I-2-3 Polenta on page 53).

SHEPHERD'S PIE

There are many different versions of shepherd's pie, but we like this one that we created on a cold, rainy evening in January. Kids love this dish served with their favorite condiment—ketchup! This shepherd's pie is even better the next day.

MAKES 8 TO 10 SERVINGS

4 to 5 medium Yukon Gold potatoes (about 2 pounds), halved

½ cup butter (1 stick), melted

½ cup buttermilk or whole milk

Salt and pepper to taste

4 tablespoons (½ stick) butter

6 to 8 large button mushrooms, cleaned and cut into thin slices

1 cup chopped yellow onion

1 medium carrot, peeled and finely chopped

1 clove garlic, peeled and finely chopped

1 tablespoon Worcestershire sauce

1 tablespoon olive oil

1½ pounds extra-lean ground beef

1 tablespoon all-purpose flour

½ teaspoon Old Bay seasoning

1 cup beef broth

One 14.5-ounce can Muir Glen diced fire-roasted tomatoes (or diced plain tomatoes), drained

¼ cup coarsely chopped Italian parsley, for garnish

☉ Preheat the oven to 350° F.

☉ In a large stockpot cover the potatoes with cold water and bring to a boil. Turn the heat down to medium and cook the potatoes until fork-tender, for about 10 minutes. Put a strainer in the sink. Remove the potatoes to the sink. Drain and allow to cool slightly. Pull the skin off the potatoes. In a large bowl mash the potatoes with a potato masher or use a potato ricer until smooth.

Add the melted butter and buttermilk and stir to blend. Season with salt and pepper and set aside.

☉ In a 5½-quart Dutch oven melt 2 tablespoons of butter over medium heat. Add the mushrooms and onions and sauté for 5 minutes. Add the carrots and garlic and sauté for 5 minutes. Add the Worcestershire and sauté for 5 minutes. Remove the mushroom mixture to a bowl and reserve.

☉ Add the olive oil and ground beef to the Dutch oven and sauté for 5 minutes, or until the meat starts to brown. Return the mushroom mixture to the pot. Mix in the flour. Add the Old Bay seasoning, salt, and pepper and stir to mix well. Stir in the beef broth and canned tomatoes. Cook for 5 minutes.

☉ Spread the mashed potatoes evenly over the top of the meat and vegetable mixture. Dot the top with the remaining 2 tablespoons butter. Transfer to the center of the oven and bake uncovered for 10 minutes. Broil for 5 minutes to brown the potatoes. Pull from the oven and sprinkle with parsley and salt. Serve in warmed shallow bowls.

ROASTED MUSSELS WITH PINOT GRIGIO

Pinot grigio has become a very popular Northwest white wine. Chill a bottle to drink along with your fresh mussels. Don't debeard them until right before cooking. Discard any mussels that are open or that won't close when pinched together before cooking.

MAKES 4 SERVINGS

> 1½ cups pinot grigio
> 2 pounds mussels, well rinsed and debearded
> 4 tablespoons (½ stick) butter, cut into ½-inch pieces
> 1 cup ¼-inch-thick crescents of white onion
> ½ lemon, cut into thin slices
> ½ cup chopped Italian parsley

◌ In a 5½-quart Dutch oven bring the wine to a boil. Boil for 2 minutes. Add the mussels, butter, and onions and cook for 5 to 7 minutes, moving the pot back and forth on the burner several times to shake the mussels. Add the lemon and parsley. The mussels should all open.

◌ Serve in shallow bowls with the broth. Provide crusty bread for dipping.

SKIMPY SHRIMP

This easy-to-prepare dish is delicious served right out of the oven. We always looked forward to eating this cheese bread soufflé at Grandma Kramis's house on Friday nights.

MAKES 6 SERVINGS

- 2 tablespoons butter
- 1½ cups half-and-half
- 4 large eggs
- 2 cups grated medium cheddar cheese
- 6 slices of French bread, cut into ½-inch cubes
- 8 ounces cooked prawns, shelled and cut into ½-inch pieces (discard the tails), or 8 ounces fully cooked small shrimp

☺ Butter the inside of a 2-quart Dutch oven. Whisk the half-and-half and eggs in a large mixing bowl. Add the cheese and bread cubes to the egg mixture, then add the prawns or shrimp. Transfer everything to the Dutch oven. Cover and refrigerate for at least 1 hour.

☺ Remove the Dutch oven from the refrigerator and let it sit for 30 minutes at room temperature. Preheat the oven to 375° F. Place the pot in the oven and bake, uncovered, until golden brown on top, for about 45 to 50 minutes. Serve right away.

BONNIE'S FISH STEW

The fresh basil adds just the right flavor to this Northwest fish stew. It's a wonderful summer dish served with melon and proscuitto. Our thanks to Bonnie for sharing this delicious recipe with us.

MAKES 6 SERVINGS

½ cup olive oil
1½ cups chopped yellow onion
4 cloves garlic, minced
2 cups white wine
Two 28-ounce cans chopped tomatoes with juice
1½ teaspoons fennel seeds
1½ teaspoons dried thyme
Pinch of saffron
Dash of red pepper flakes
Salt and pepper to taste
1 Dungeness crab, cleaned and cracked
2 pounds mussels, debearded
1 pound prawns, cleaned
2 pounds firm white fish (such as snapper or cod), cut into 3-inch pieces
Fresh basil, chopped, for garnish
Fresh parsley, chopped, for garnish

⊘ In a 5-quart Dutch oven, heat oil over medium-low heat. Add onions and cook for 5 minutes. Add garlic and wine. Cook 5 minutes. Add tomatoes, juice, and spices. Simmer for 20 minutes. Add seafood. Cover and cook for 5–7 minutes. Serve in large bowls. Sprinkle each bowl of stew with parsley and basil and serve.

ACCOMPANIMENTS

III

You will find yourself making these accompaniments in large quantities because they disappear so quickly. We always keep them on hand, refrigerated or in the freezer. The Picadillo, Caponata, Red Onion Jam, Chunky Applesauce, Chunky Mango Chutney, and Rhubarb Compote make great gifts for friends and family. The Chunky Mango Chutney simmers in the Dutch oven until it glistens and the sweet, tangy flavors develop. Serve as a condiment with roast chicken or pork roast. The rose-colored Rhubarb Compote with a touch of star-anise flavor is a taste of spring served warm over vanilla ice cream or on top of grilled fresh halibut. The Dutch oven is a magic pot that blends the flavors and brightens the colors of everything cooked in it.

GINNY GROSSI'S RAGÙ SAUCE

This quick to prepare and delicious sauce, created by our dear friend Ginny, coats the noodles. It's not chunky, and it doesn't fall off onto your plate. Serve with garlic bread and a bowl of freshly grated Parmesan cheese.

MAKES 6 SERVINGS

2 tablespoons olive oil

¼ cup finely diced yellow onion

I clove garlic, peeled and minced

I pound lean ground beef

8 ounces ground pork sausage

Two 15-ounce cans tomato sauce

¼ teaspoon dried Italian seasoning

I bay leaf

I tablespoon dried basil

I tablespoon sugar

I cup grated Parmesan cheese, for serving

⏾ Heat the olive oil in a 5½-quart Dutch oven over medium heat. Sauté the onions and garlic for about 5 minutes, or until the onions are soft. Add the beef and pork sausage to the onion mixture and cook until lightly browned, stirring gently. With a wooden spoon break up the ground beef and sausage into small pieces.

⏾ Add the tomato sauce, Italian seasoning, bay leaf, basil, and sugar. Simmer uncovered over low heat for 1½ hours. Give the sauce an occasional stir every time you walk by. Don't add salt—this sauce does not need it. If the sauce is too thick or salty, add ¾ cup water.

Note: One pound of spaghetti will be the right amount for this recipe. Drop the noodles in a large pot of boiling, salted water (use 3 tablespoons salt for 6 to 8 quarts of water). Cook just until the noodles are soft, for about 8 minutes, being careful not to overcook. Immediately add 1 cup of cold water to stop the cooking and then drain well in a colander. Place the noodles in a large serving bowl that has been warmed slightly by rinsing with hot water and dried completely. Add 2 cups of the hot spaghetti sauce to the noodles and mix until the noodles are well coated. Add 2 more cups of sauce and mix well, then pour the remaining sauce over the top. Serve in warmed pasta bowls. Sprinkle with Parmesan cheese.

PARMESAN TOASTS

These toasts are a crisp accompaniment to serve with bean soups. We like to break the toasts into the soup.

MAKES 18 TOASTS

I small baguette, cut into 10 to 12 ½-inch slices
¼ cup olive oil
½ cup freshly grated Parmesan cheese

⊘ Put the baguette slices on a baking sheet and toast each slice under the broiler. When both sides are toasted, brush one side lightly with the olive oil and sprinkle with the Parmesan cheese. Broil just until the cheese melts and begins to brown. Serve right away with your soup of the day.

PESTO

This recipe was given to us by a good friend from Milano, Italy. His mother made the best pesto, and she always used a little yogurt to make the pesto creamy.

MAKES ABOUT 2 CUPS

    3 cloves garlic, peeled
    ½ cup (4 ounces) pine nuts
    2 ounces Parmigiano-Reggiano cheese, coarsely grated
    I teaspoon salt
    ½ teaspoon black pepper
    3 cups loosely packed fresh basil leaves, stemmed
    2 tablespoons lemon juice
    2 tablespoons plain yogurt
    ⅔ cup extra-virgin olive oil

๑ With a food processor running, add the garlic and finely chop. Stop the processor and add the pine nuts, Parmigiano-Reggiano, salt, pepper, basil, lemon juice, and yogurt. Process until blended. With the motor running, slowly add the olive oil until blended.

๑ Serve on top of hearty soups like ribollita or pasta fagioli. We also love to spread fresh pesto on fresh bread with a light spread of goat cheese, then top with a dollop of pesto.

Note: Pesto can be frozen for up to 6 weeks.

PICADILLO

This is a great filling for pita pockets: Create an easy grab-and-go lunch by serving with apples and giant cookies.

MAKES FILLING FOR 8 PITA POCKETS

2 tablespoons vegetable oil

2 cups finely chopped yellow onions

3 cloves garlic, peeled and minced

2 pounds ground beef

One 28-ounce can crushed tomatoes in purée

One 8-ounce can tomato paste

2 tablespoons brown sugar

½ cup dried currants

1 cup chopped pimento-stuffed green olives

2 tablespoons chili powder

8 pita pockets, cut in half, for serving

Shredded iceberg lettuce, for serving

⌒ Heat the vegetable oil over medium-low heat in a 5½-quart Dutch oven. Add the onions and garlic and cook for several minutes, stirring often. Add the ground beef, breaking it up into small pieces with a large wooden spoon as it cooks. Spoon out any excess liquid after the meat is partially cooked. Don't cook it longer than 5 minutes. Add the tomatoes, tomato paste, brown sugar, currants, green olives, and chili powder. Simmer uncovered over low heat for 1 hour.

⌒ Serve the filling warm, stuffed into the pita pockets on top of the shredded lettuce.

**THE
DUTCH
OVEN
COOKBOOK**

RED ONION JAM

This sweet and sour onion jam is delicious served on top of crostini that have been spread with fresh chèvre or soft, herbed cheese. It also makes a nice condiment to serve with pot roast. Stored in airtight containers, it will last about 2 weeks in the refrigerator or up to 6 weeks in the freezer.

MAKES ABOUT 3 CUPS

¼ cup olive oil

6 medium red onions (about 3 pounds), cut into thin slices

½ cup balsamic vinegar

½ cup brown sugar

I teaspoon sea salt

½ cup red wine

⊘ Heat the olive oil in a 5½-quart Dutch oven over medium heat. Add the onions, then pour in the balsamic vinegar. Stir in the brown sugar, salt, and red wine. Reduce the heat to low and simmer uncovered for 30 minutes. Stir occasionally. The onions will soften but hold their shape. Serve warm or at room temperature.

CAPONATA

The sweet and sour flavors of this braised vegetable condiment make it a nice accompaniment for grilled or roasted meats. Caponata is also a nice addition to an antipasti platter alongside meats and cheeses.

MAKES 8 SERVINGS

2 large eggplants, peeled and diced into small cubes

¾ cup olive oil

4 cloves garlic, peeled and finely chopped

1 medium yellow onion, diced

2 medium red bell peppers, stemmed, seeded, and cut into ¼-inch pieces

2 medium yellow bell peppers, stemmed, seeded, and cut into ¼-inch pieces

1 cup chopped pimento-stuffed green olives

¼ cup drained capers

¼ cup red wine vinegar

¼ cup sugar

One 28-ounce can diced tomatoes in purée

꙾ Preheat the oven to 350° F. In a large bowl, toss the eggplant pieces with ½ cup of the olive oil. Spread the oil-coated eggplant on a baking sheet and roast for 25 minutes.

꙾ In a 5½-quart Dutch oven heat add the remaining ¼ cup olive oil over medium-low heat. Sauté the garlic, onion, and peppers. Add the green olives, capers, red wine vinegar, sugar, and tomatoes in purée and turn the heat down to low. Simmer uncovered for 15 minutes. Add the roasted eggplant to the tomato mixture, stir gently, and simmer for 15 minutes longer. Serve at room temperature.

CHUNKY APPLESAUCE

When making applesauce, we like to pair Winesap or Jonagold apples with the Braeburn variety (Winesaps and Jonagolds break down a bit more than Braeburns do). The natural sweetness of the Braeburns and the tartness of the Winesaps or Jonagolds complement each other. We rely on the fruit for the sweetness and avoid adding too much sugar.

MAKES 6 SERVINGS

3 Winesap or Jonagold apples, peeled and coarsely chopped

3 Braeburn apples, peeled and coarsely chopped

1 cup water

¼ cup sugar

Juice of 1 orange, plus two 1-inch strips of orange zest

1 cinnamon stick

⅛ teaspoon grated nutmeg

⅛ teaspoon allspice

Dash of ground cinnamon

In a 5½-quart Dutch oven add the apples, water, sugar, orange juice, orange zest, and the spices. Cook over medium-low heat with the lid off for 45 minutes, stirring occasionally. Serve warm or at room temperature alongside a pork roast or pork chops.

CHUNKY MANGO CHUTNEY

*This is a favorite family recipe that we always have on hand in the
refrigerator to accompany roast chicken or pork. Everything goes into the
Dutch oven at the same time and then slowly simmers for 1½ to 2 hours.*

MAKES 6 CUPS

¼ cup olive oil

4 cups chopped yellow onion

3 large cloves garlic, peeled and minced

3 pounds frozen mango cubes

I red bell pepper, stemmed, seeded, and finely diced

I cup dried currants

¼ cup peeled and finely diced fresh ginger

I tablespoon mustard seeds

I teaspoon crushed red pepper flakes

I teaspoon ground turmeric

I lime, cut into quarters and thin slices

Juice of I lemon

2 cups apple cider vinegar

I pound light brown sugar

3 cinnamon sticks

↺ Heat the olive oil over medium heat in a 5½-quart Dutch oven. Put the
onions, garlic, mango, red bell pepper, currants, and ginger into the pot.
Add the mustard seeds, red pepper flakes, turmeric, lime, lemon juice, apple
cider vinegar, brown sugar, and cinnamon sticks. Heat the mixture for 10
minutes, stirring frequently. Then turn the heat down to low and simmer
uncovered for 1½ hours, until the mixture thickens and has a shiny appear-
ance. Cool.

↺ Remove the cinnamon sticks. Freeze in half-pint containers until ready to
use. The chutney will last for several weeks in the refrigerator.

SPICED RED WINE

There are many different versions of spiced or mulled red wine, served hot. In Germany it is called gluhwein, *the French name is* vin chaud, *and the Italian name is* vin brule. *Our good friends from Sweden make their own version, called glögg, which has almonds and raisins in it. It is wonderful after a day of skiing or playing in the snow.*

MAKES 20 SERVINGS

2 whole cinnamon sticks

1 medium orange, studded with 8 whole cloves

2 strips of lemon zest (about ½ inch wide)

8 whole allspice berries

2 bottles medium- to full-bodied red wine

¾ cup water

½ cup sugar

½ cup Cognac, brandy, or Grand Marnier

⊘ In a 5½-quart Dutch oven, add the cinnamon sticks, orange with cloves, lemon zest, allspice berries, red wine, water, and sugar. Heat the mixture gently over low heat. *Do not boil!* Heat for 45 minutes, stirring occasionally to make sure the sugar has dissolved. Using a large slotted spoon, remove the orange. Add the Cognac and heat for 5 minutes longer.

⊘ Ladle into warmed mugs. Keep the remaining spiced wine warm in the Dutch oven over low heat.

RHUBARB COMPOTE

This is wonderful as a savory or sweet accompaniment. We love it with pork tenderloin, fresh halibut, or on top of vanilla ice cream drizzled with the warm syrup that is left behind after straining the rhubarb.

MAKES 2 CUPS COMPOTE

I pound rhubarb, rinsed, trimmed (cut about I inch off tops and bottoms of stalks), and cut into ½-inch pieces (4 cups)

2 cups water

⅔ cup sugar

I cinnamon stick

2 pieces of star anise

2 ¼-inch slices fresh ginger

⊘ Add the chopped rhubarb to the Dutch oven. Add the water and the sugar and stir. Add the cinnamon stick, star anise, and ginger. Cover the pot and cook over medium heat until the liquid starts to boil, about 5 minutes. Turn down the heat to low and cook for 10 minutes or until the rhubarb just starts to fall apart but is still holding its shape.

⊘ With a fine-mesh strainer, strain the compote over a large bowl. Discard the cinnamon stick, star anise, ginger, and orange zest.

⊘ Place in a bowl and serve on top of or alongside pork, fish, or ice cream. Save the syrup that is left in the bowl, and if you want the syrup to thicken, just place it back on the burner over medium heat and cook down until syrup starts to thicken. Save both the compote and the syrup in the refrigerator for up to 3 weeks or freeze.

DESSERTS

Apple Brown Betty
Roasted Red Pears
Cinnamon Rice Pudding
Peach Melba
Lemon Cake Pudding with Blueberries
Toasted Almond and Apricot Bread Pudding
Spudnuts with Cardamom Syrup
Sticky Toffee Dessert
Sopaipillas
Beignets

oasted Red Pears, Apple Brown Betty, and Cinnamon Rice Pudding are all perfect for the Dutch oven because it conducts heat so evenly. The Toasted Almond and Apricot Bread Pudding and Sticky Toffee Dessert get a wonderful golden crust. We like to serve these moist, old-fashioned desserts in our grandmother's cut-glass dishes topped with whipped cream.

Whether you are frying, poaching, roasting, or baking, you will find success in the Dutch oven. The Sopaipillas (mini doughnuts) are always a hit with the children. Don't be afraid to deep-fry over medium heat in your Dutch oven. Just be sure not to let your oil get too hot, and only fry in 2 to 3 inches of safflower or peanut oil.

APPLE BROWN BETTY

This is such an easy autumn dessert. The toasted crumbs add flavor and texture. Bake this apple treat in a 2-quart Dutch oven. Serve warm topped with vanilla ice cream.

MAKES 6 SERVINGS

3 cups coarse bread crumbs, toasted

½ cup butter (1 stick), melted

1¼ cups sugar

½ teaspoon ground cinnamon

3 large Cameo or Braeburn apples, peeled, cored, quartered, and cut crosswise into ¼-inch slices

↺ Preheat the oven to 350° F. In a medium-sized bowl, mix the toasted bread crumbs with half of the butter, ¼ cup of the sugar, and the cinnamon. In another medium-sized bowl, mix the apples, the rest of the butter, and the remaining 1 cup sugar.

↺ Layer the bread crumb–butter mixture and the apple-sugar-butter mixture in the Dutch oven as follows: Spread a third of the crumb mixture over the bottom of the pot. Add half of the apples and another third of the crumb mixture. Add the rest of the apples and sprinkle the remaining third of the crumbs over it all.

↺ Place the Dutch oven inside the oven and bake uncovered for 50 minutes. Serve warm.

ROASTED RED PEARS

This is a memorable dessert served after a delicious dinner on a moonlit October evening. October at the farmers market features freshly picked pears—choose Bosc pears, which are the best for baking.

MAKES 6 SERVINGS

I tablespoon salted butter

1¼ cups sugar

5 Jonagold apples, peeled, cored, and chopped

3 tablespoons chopped walnuts

I cup red wine

I cinnamon stick

I strip of lemon zest

6 Bosc pears, peeled but not cored

I pint heavy cream, whipped with 2 tablespoons sugar

☺ In a medium-sized saucepan melt the butter over medium-low heat with ¼ cup of the sugar. Add the apples, cover, and cook until soft, for about 10 minutes. Remove from the heat and add the walnuts. Set aside.

☺ In a 5½-quart Dutch oven bring the red wine and the remaining 1 cup sugar to a boil. Add the cinnamon stick and lemon zest. Turn the heat down to a simmer. Cut the bottom of each pear so they stand upright in the Dutch oven. Cover and gently simmer for 30 to 40 minutes, until tender. Gently pierce with the tip of a small paring knife to test for doneness. Remove the pears to a platter.

☺ Turn the heat to medium and reduce the sugar and wine mixture to a thick glaze. Serve in individual dessert dishes. Place a little of the apple mixture in each dish and set a cooked pear on top. Spoon a little glaze over each pear. Serve with the whipped cream.

CINNAMON RICE PUDDING

We like our rice pudding without raisins, but you can add them if you like. Be sure to presoak them in boiling water and drain before including. This easy custard pudding can be quickly assembled, especially if you have leftover cooked white rice.. This old-fashioned dessert is good any time of day—we even like it for breakfast.

MAKES 6 SERVINGS

I tablespoon butter

2 cups cooked white rice

½ teaspoon ground cinnamon

¾ cup sugar

5 large eggs, beaten

2 cups heavy cream

I teaspoon vanilla extract

Sprinkle of ground cinnamon, for garnish

Heavy cream, for serving

⌒ Preheat the oven to 350° F. Butter the inside of a 2-quart Dutch oven and put the rice in the pot.

⌒ In a large bowl, mix the cinnamon, sugar, and eggs until well blended. Whisk in the cream and vanilla. Pour the mixture gently over the rice. Cover with the lid and place the Dutch oven in the oven. Bake for 50 minutes, or until the custard is set. Remove from the oven and sprinkle lightly with cinnamon.

⌒ Serve warm with chilled cream poured over.

Note: Refrigerate any leftovers—this dessert tastes great served cold the next day.

PEACH MELBA

This delicious dessert was created in 1893 by Auguste Escoffier at the Savoy Hotel in London. Escoffier made this special dessert for a party to celebrate opera singer Dame Nellie Melba's visit to London. We have adapted this recipe to include cardamon and fresh blackberries or marionberries. Serve with vanilla ice cream or fresh whipped cream. You can also add a sprig of mint to each dish.

MAKES 6 SERVINGS

6 medium firm-ripe peaches

Poaching Liquid

1⅓ cups sugar

2 cups water

2 teaspoons vanilla extract or ½ fresh vanilla bean

6 whole green cardamon pods (see note)

Raspberry Sauce

½ cup sugar

⅓ cup water

One 12-ounce package frozen raspberries or 3 cups fresh blackberries or marionberries

2 teaspoons fresh lemon juice

⊘ Bring 2 quarts of water to a boil in a 5½-quart Dutch oven. Add the peaches and cook for 1 minute. Remove them with a slotted spoon to a bowl of ice water to stop the cooking. Transfer the peaches to a cutting board and peel, starting at the end that has the "X." Cut the peaches in half and remove and discard the pits. Pour out the water remaining in the Dutch oven.

⊘ For the poaching liquid, add the sugar, water, vanilla, and cardamon pods to the Dutch oven. Bring the mixture to a boil and stir with a wooden spoon until the sugar has dissolved. Gently add the peach halves to the poaching liquid, then reduce the heat and simmer uncovered for 5 minutes. Turn the peaches over and cook for 5 minutes more. Cool the peaches in the poaching liquid for 1 hour.

- For the berry sauce, bring the water and sugar to a boil in a medium-sized saucepan over medium heat, stirring occasionally. Turn the heat down to low and add the berries. Cook for 10 minutes. Place a fine-mesh strainer over a bowl and pour the berry syrup into the strainer, pushing down with the back of a spatula to squeeze out any juice from the berries. Discard the pulp, and cool the berry purée in the refrigerator for 1 hour.

- Stir in the lemon juice. Serve the peaches in a glass bowl or sundae dish. Add a scoop of ice cream or whipped cream to the center of each peach. Drizzle with blackberry purée.

Note: If you are using fresh vanilla bean in the poaching liquid, scrape the seeds into the Dutch oven, then add the whole pod. Also, if you have a hard time finding whole green cardamom pods, you can substitute 3 star anise.

LEMON CAKE PUDDING WITH BLUEBERRIES

This light dessert is a perfect finish to a salmon dinner. It separates into a cake on the top and a pudding underneath.

MAKES 6 SERVINGS

3 eggs, separated
3 tablespoons all-purpose flour
I cup sugar
I tablespoon butter, melted
6 tablespoons lemon juice
I teaspoon grated lemon zest
1¼ cups milk
Whipped cream, for garnish
Fresh blueberries, for garnish

☽ Preheat the oven to 350° F.

☽ In a large bowl, beat the egg whites until stiff. Beat the egg yolks in another large bowl, and add the flour and sugar. Add the butter, lemon juice, lemon zest, and milk. Fold in the egg whites.

☽ Pour the mixture into a 2-quart Dutch oven and bake uncovered for 40 minutes, or until the pudding is set. Serve with whipped cream and fresh blueberries.

TOASTED ALMOND AND
APRICOT BREAD PUDDING

This bread pudding gets a nice crust all the way around when prepared in a Dutch oven, leaving the center moist. Serve warm with lightly whipped cream. The hint of Triple Sec is a nice flavor with the apricots.

MAKES 10 SERVINGS

I medium loaf egg bread with crust (challah or brioche), cut into I½-inch cubes (about 8 cups)

2 tablespoons butter

6 large eggs, whole

2 large egg yolks

I cup granulated sugar

3½ cups half-and-half

2 teaspoons vanilla extract

¼ teaspoon ground nutmeg

3 tablespoons Triple Sec or orange liqueur

½ cup slivered almonds, toasted

8 ounces ripe apricots, chopped

Powdered sugar, for garnish

Whipped cream, for serving

⊘ Arrange the bread cubes in a single layer on 2 baking sheets. Let stand at room temperature uncovered to dry overnight.

⊘ Preheat the oven to 375° F. Butter a 5½-quart Dutch oven with 2 tablespoons butter.

⊘ Using an electric mixer, beat the eggs and egg yolks in a large bowl until frothy. Add the granulated sugar and beat for 5 minutes on medium-high speed, until the mixture thickens and becomes pale yellow. Add the half-and-half, vanilla, nutmeg, and Triple Sec and beat just until blended.

⊙ Add half of the bread cubes to the Dutch oven. Sprinkle on half of the almonds and apricots. Pour half of the custard mixture into the Dutch oven. Add the rest of the bread cubes, apricots, and almonds. Pour the remaining custard over the top. Press gently with the back of a spatula, making sure the bread cubes are submerged. Let stand for 10 minutes.

⊙ Cover the Dutch oven, place in the oven, and bake for 20 minutes. Press down the bread–custard mixture with the back of the spatula, then bake for another 25 minutes. A knife inserted in the center should come out clean; the bread pudding should be golden brown on the sides and on top. Let stand for 5 minutes. Sprinkle with powdered sugar. Serve warm in heated dessert bowls, topped with whipped cream.

SPUDNUTS WITH CARDAMOM SYRUP

We have enjoyed these at several Indian restaurants, and we have finally duplicated our own version of this delicious yet simple treat. The doughnuts soak up the syrup and are the perfect ending to a meal, served with a cup of chai tea.

MAKES 24 MINI DOUGHNUTS

Spudnuts

    I cup heavy cream
    ½ cup plus 3 tablespoons all-purpose flour
    ½ cup milk
    2 cups vegetable oil, for frying

Cardamom Syrup

    3 cups water
    3 cups sugar
    IO whole green cardamom pods

⊙ To prepare the doughnuts, combine the heavy cream, flour, and milk in a large mixing bowl. Stir well for a few minutes until a smooth paste forms. Let rest for I5 minutes.

⊙ Meanwhile, heat the oil in a Dutch oven over medium-high heat, until the oil is 375° F. Drop in small teaspoon-sized balls of dough. Fry IO to I2 doughnuts at a time. Carefully spoon hot oil over the tops. Cook until golden brown, for about 2 minutes on each side, then remove with a slotted spoon to a paper towel–lined plate.

⊙ To prepare the syrup, bring the water, sugar, and cardamom pods to a boil over high heat in a small, heavy saucepan. Cook covered for about 5 minutes. Reduce the heat to medium and cook uncovered for IO more minutes. Remove from the heat and let steep for I5 minutes. Strain the syrup into a medium-sized bowl.

⊙ Serve in separate dessert bowls. Place 6 spudnuts to a dish and pour ¼ cup syrup over the tops.

THE
DUTCH
OVEN
COOKBOOK

STICKY TOFFEE DESSERT

The dates make this dessert moist, but even if you are not fond of dates you will be pleasantly surprised. It's hard to tell they are even there. Top it off with a little of the caramel sauce and whipped cream.

MAKES 6 TO 8 SERVINGS

Caramel Sauce

> 1 cup unsalted butter (2 sticks)
> 1¾ cups brown sugar
> 1 cup heavy cream

Toffee Pudding

> 6 ounces chopped and pitted dates
> 1 teaspoon baking soda
> 1¼ cups boiling water
> ¼ cup unsalted butter (½ stick), softened
> ½ cup brown sugar, firmly packed
> 1 teaspoon vanilla extract
> 1 egg
> 1½ cups all-purpose flour
> 1½ teaspoons baking powder

↺ To make the sauce, melt the butter over medium-high heat in a medium-sized saucepan. Add the brown sugar and the cream. Bring the mixture to a boil, then turn the heat down and simmer for 5 minutes, until the mixture browns and thickens slightly. Pour half of the caramel sauce into a 2-quart Dutch oven. Reserve the rest to pour over the pudding just before serving.

↺ Preheat the oven to 350° F.

↺ To prepare the pudding, place the chopped dates in a medium-sized bowl with the baking soda. Pour the boiling water over the dates and allow to cool to room temperature.

⊘ Meanwhile in a separate mixing bowl, combine the butter, brown sugar, and vanilla and beat with an electric mixer until the mixture is creamed. Beat in the egg and stir in the date mixture. In a small bowl mix together the flour and baking powder, then fold into the egg mixture until everything is combined.

⊘ Pour the pudding batter into the Dutch oven with the sauce, cover with the lid, place on a baking sheet, and bake in the oven for 30 minutes. Decrease the oven temperature to 325° F and cook uncovered for another 60 minutes.

⊘ Serve the pudding warm with the reserved caramel sauce and some whipped cream spooned over the top.

Frying

You can shallow-fry in the Dutch oven (using about 2 inches of oil) because it is deep enough and provides a good source of even heat. Keep the oil temperature at 360° to 375° F. We like to use peanut oil for frying because of its high smoke point. Use a bamboo-handled strainer to remove the finished fried foods, drain well, and always season while hot. Let the hot oil cool to room temperature, pour it into an empty jar, and discard. We have found that saving oil to reuse is *not* a good idea. The oil turns rancid quickly after it has been heated. In addition, small burnt particles can result in an off flavor. You don't want apple fritters that taste like onion rings, right?

SOPAIPILLAS

These puffed fritters are a family favorite. Whether a grown-up or a child is enjoying them, these tasty treats will quickly disappear. Dust with powdered sugar or drizzle with honey.

MAKES 20 SOPAIPILLAS

2 cups all-purpose flour

2 teaspoons double-acting baking powder

I teaspoon salt

2 tablespoons vegetable shortening

¾ cup water

6 cups vegetable oil, for frying

1½ teaspoons ground cinnamon

¼ cup sugar

⟳ In a medium-sized bowl sift together the flour, baking powder, and salt. Add the shortening and mix until it has the consistency of coarse cornmeal. Stir in the water; add enough to form the mixture into a soft dough. Lightly knead the dough on a floured surface. Add a little more flour if the dough is sticking. Roll it out to ¹⁄₁₆ inch thick. Cut the dough into 3-inch squares and cover with a damp dish towel.

⟳ In a 5½-quart Dutch oven add enough oil, about 6 cups, to measure 2 inches in depth. Heat until a frying thermometer reaches 375° F. Fry the squares in batches, for I minute on each side, until golden and puffed. Transfer with a slotted spoon to a paper towel–lined plate.

⟳ In a small paper bag shake the sopaipillas together with the cinnamon and sugar. Keep them warm before serving in a 250° F oven.

BEIGNETS

The best beignets I have ever had are the ones my mom made growing up. However, those from Café Du Monde in New Orleans, Louisiana, are a close second. Beignets are traditionally made with a choux pastry and deep-fried until golden brown. They are then doused with powdered sugar and devoured with a café au lait. Kids love these with fresh strawberry jam or orange honey butter.

MAKES 30 BEIGNETS

¾ cup warm water (100–115° F)

1 package active dry yeast

¼ cup sugar

½ teaspoon salt

1 large egg

½ cup evaporated milk

3½ cups flour

3 tablespoons softened butter

1 quart vegetable oil, for frying

1 cup confectioners' sugar for dusting

↻ Pour the warm water into a large bowl, sprinkle in the yeast, and add 2 teaspoons of the sugar. Stir until dissolved. Let sit and proof for 10 minutes. Add the remaining sugar, salt, egg, and evaporated milk. Gradually stir in 2 cups of the flour and beat with a wooden spoon until smooth and thoroughly blended. Beat in the butter, then add the remaining flour. Beat it in with a spoon until it becomes too stiff to stir, and work in the rest with your hands. Put the dough into a greased bowl, cover with plastic wrap, and refrigerate overnight.

↻ Preheat the oven to 200° F. On a lightly-floured board, roll the dough out to about ⅛ inch, and cut 2½- by 3½-inch pieces with a sharp knife. Heat the vegetable oil in a 5½-quart Dutch oven to 360° F. When it reaches the desired temperature, turn the heat down slightly. Fry the beignets in batches of 4, turning them over a few times until they puff up and are golden brown on both sides (about 2-3 minutes per batch). Remove with a slotted spoon to layers of paper towels, then transfer to your preheated oven until all the beignets are finished. Sprinkle generously with powdered sugar, and serve on a platter or on dessert plates.

RESOURCES

Amazon.com
Pomegranate molasses, Crystal's hot sauce (also found at specialty food stores)

Bob's Red Mill Natural Foods, Inc.
5209 SE International Way
Milwaukie, OR 97222
503-654-3215
www.bobsredmill.com
Grains, cornmeal

Crate and Barrel
800-967-6696
www.crateandbarrel.com
Enameled Dutch ovens and other kitchen equipment

Importfood.com
888-618-THAI, ext. 8424
Coconut milk, Thai chile pastes, Thai curry pastes, Three Crab fish sauce, fresh Thai produce, kaffir lime leaves, lemongrass, Thai basil

Lodge Manufacturing Company
P.O. Box 380
South Pittsburg, TN 37380
423-837-7181
www.lodgemfg.com
Our preferred supplier of cast iron cookware

More Than Gourmet
800-860-9385
www.morethangourmet.com
Demi-glaces, stocks, and other sauces

Saltworks
18080 NE 68th Street, Suite A-150
Redmond, WA 98052
425-885-7258
sales@saltworks.us, www.saltworks.us
Fleur de sel, Murray River sea salt, smoked sea salts, and other types of salt

Staub USA, Inc.
115 Pine Avenue, Suite 640
Long Beach, CA 90802
866-782-8287
www.staubusa.com
Beautiful and unique cast iron pieces from France

Sur la Table
84 Pine Street
Seattle, WA 98101
800-243-0852
www.surlatable.com
Lodge, Staub, and Le Creuset enameled and nonenameled cast iron pieces as well as a large range of cookware

Washington State University Creamery
101 Food Quality Building
P.O. Box 641122
Pullman, WA 99161-1122
800-457-5442
www.wsu.edu/creamery/cougarcheese/1flavors.html
Cougar Gold cheese

World Spice Merchants
1509 Western Avenue
Seattle, WA 98101
206-682-7274
www.worldspice.com
Fresh spices and spice blends, such as garam masala, curry powder, cardamom, and star anise

INDEX

**THE
DUTCH
OVEN
COOKBOOK**

ABOUT THE AUTHORS

Harker Hearne

Sharon Kramis *(right)* is the author of three cookbooks, *Northwest Bounty*, *Berries: A Country Garden Cookbook*, and co-author of *The Cast Iron Skillet Cookbook*. A Northwest native, she holds a degree in food science from the University of Washington and is a former food writer for the *Mercer Island Reporter*. Sharon studied with legendary cooking figure James Beard at his summer cooking school in Seaside, Oregon, for six years. She is a founding member of the International Association of Culinary Professionals, Les Dames d'Escoffier's Seattle chapter, and FareStart, a program that trains homeless persons for the hospitality industry. In addition to participating in menu development for Anthony's Restaurants in Seattle, Sharon continues to educate herself through travel and ongoing classes at the California Culinary Academy in Napa Valley. She lives with her husband, Larry, in Seattle.

Julie Kramis Hearne *(left)* is co-author of *The Cast Iron Skillet Cookbook*. She was brought up with a love for food. When she was young, she would pretend to be sick so she could stay home from school and watch her mother teach cooking classes, and she often accompanied her mother to James Beard's cooking classes. The former owner of two Seattle restaurants, Julie has worked as a restaurant consultant and spent a year learning at the nationally renowned Herbfarm Restaurant in Woodinville, Washington. Julie is a member of Women Chefs and Restaurateurs, the International Association of Culinary Professionals, and Women for Wine Sense, and is currently on the board of Slow Food. She continues to learn about food through ongoing classes at the California Culinary Academy in Napa Valley. She lives with her husband, Harker, and two young sons in Seattle. Visit Julie's website at www.whatisjuliemaking.com.